Also by Allysa Torey

The Magnolia Bakery Cookbook (with Jennifer Appel)

More from
Magnolia

RECIPES FROM THE WORLD-FAMOUS BAKERY
AND ALLYSA TOREY'S HOME KITCHEN

Allysa Torey

SIMON & SCHUSTER
New York London Toronto Sydney

SIMON & SCHUSTER
Rockefeller Center
1230 Avenue of the Americas
New York, NY 10020

For information about special discounts for bulk purchases,
please contact Simon & Schuster Special Sales:
1-800-465-6798 or business@simonandschuster.com.

Designed by Jaime Putorti

Manufactured in the United States of America

20 19 18 17 16 15 14 13 12

Library of Congress Cataloging-in-Publication Data
Torey, Allysa.
    More from Magnolia : recipes from the world-famous bakery and Allysa Torey's home kitchen.
    p. cm.
    1. Baking. 2. Desserts. 3. Magolia Bakery. I. Title.
    TX765.T67 2004
    641.8'15—dc22

                                                          2004045222

ISBN 0-7432-4661-6

For Tadhg,

who says I could never make anything that wasn't good
and whose love helps make my dreams come true

Acknowledgments

I would like to thank my agent, Carla Glasser, and my editor, Sydny Miner, for convincing me to write a second book when I didn't think I wanted to. It turned out to be a very wonderful and creative experience. Special thanks to Barbara DiNicola and my managing staff at Magnolia, whose incredible hard work and support enabled me to take the opportunity to put this project together; and thanks particularly to Margaret Hathaway for her contributions and her assistance and computer skills. Lastly, I would like to thank our loyal customers who have continued to support us over the years despite the crazy long lines out the door.

Contents

Foreword

$\mathcal{A}$ cupcake can change your life. That was an epiphany to which I was not privy in the summer of 1996. Theater and art are my calling, but in the creative tradition, I needed rent money to sustain those passions. I walked into Magnolia Bakery. I cannot imagine walking out.

On a quiet corner in the residential heart of the West Village, I have played a part in the theater of sugared success, family dynamic, and New York renown. Cherished customers looked wistfully to that first summer when there was no limit on cupcakes per person, when lines never wrapped around the block, when the nightly staff was Allysa, my sister Shelly, and myself. Visit today, and the cast has quadrupled, the baking is unremitting, and as many as five people have the sole task of icing cupcakes. Yet while the number of people who enter the store has changed drastically, the store has not. Frequently I am asked about expansion, I just smile. The real thing happens but once.

Magnolia Bakery is tradition. Oh, yes, the business is young, but what is inside is ageless. How beautiful that American tradition thrives in a city known for people who left tradition behind, in a bakery that is alternately Grandma's kitchen and a happening hot spot. It is a place where success has been earned through hard work, where the kitchen is right before your eyes and baking from scratch is priority, and where wealth or fame must wait on line with everybody else.

Because of Magnolia, many of us in the City have a place where every season is joy again. This past holiday a former employee who had left to become a trapeze artist came straight from the airport to Magnolia. How can I not take pride in such a workplace? Although this vision was not my own, I delight at the result of combined efforts. With Allysa's family and my own as colleagues, we have worked through proposals, discoveries, friendships, and love gained and lost—all while we are ever mixing, measuring, scooping, and icing . . . forever icing. You can work with your family, and sometimes the people you work with become family, and sometimes becoming passionate about the way you earn your rent can change you. This began as a bit part, and I now find myself in the director's chair, lending what I learn to everything else.

Sometimes when I turn the corner of West 11th Street to another night of sweet chaos, it surprises me, not yet or ever immune. It is the smell of cake baking, I am at work, and I am at home.

Barbara DiNicola

Magnolia General Manager

September 2004

Introduction

*W*hen we first opened the Magnolia Bakery, I imagined a cozy, old-fashioned shop where people could come for a cup of coffee and something sweet. I expected our customers to include some local regulars and lots of neighborhood families. I thought we'd close at seven each evening so I could go home and make dinner. I never expected that Magnolia would turn into a city-wide hangout, much less that on weekend nights there would be lines out the door!

The bakery is busier now than ever. Our customers stop by as much for the feel of the store as they do for the desserts. With its vintage American decor and desserts, customers often tell me that walking into the bakery is just like stepping back in time to their grandmother's kitchen. They come in for a slice of cake and end up with a little piece of their childhood. Many want to meet me to say thanks for making the red velvet cake they remember from church picnics or the banana pudding just like their mom used to make.

Since the publication of *The Magnolia Bakery Cookbook,* many people have suggested that I do a second book. While working full-time at the bakery, the idea of writing another cookbook seemed impossible. Finally, after putting together a committed staff at the shop, we were able to move full-time to our country house, and I could really consider the idea, knowing that I would have the time and energy necessary to write the book I wanted to write.

The kitchen in my house is the one I've always dreamed of having. It's a big country kitchen with a window over the double white enamel sink that looks out on my vegetable garden and the cornfields beyond. The walls are painted pale yellow, and the glass-fronted cabinets, filled with vintage dishware and linens, are a creamy white. I have a counter just for baking that holds my 1950s Sunbeam Mixmaster, and there is a big enamel table that sits in the middle of the room, which is the perfect place for rolling out piecrusts.

Being able to work on the book in the country has turned out to be a wonderful experience. It's been great to be able to work on ideas for recipes while sitting on the back porch and then go straight into the kitchen to try them out. I like to create recipes in an old-fashioned style, but with new ideas and perhaps different combinations of ingredients to keep things interesting and fun.

These classic American desserts reflect the sensibilities of the bakery and my home. They aren't fussy or difficult—they're simply my favorites.

Allysa Torey
September 2004

More from Magnolia

Helpful Hints

Since the first cookbook was published, I've received many, many phone calls from all over the country, and I have frequently been approached at the bakery with questions about specific recipes and baking tips in general. Because of this I've gone over the original Helpful Hints section and tried to go into more depth in areas that might be especially useful to the home baker.

General Baking Hints

At the bakery, even while producing large quantities of desserts, we always use the best and freshest ingredients, and we adhere to a set procedure every time.

Before starting it is important to read through the recipe from beginning to end to ensure that you understand it thoroughly. Then assemble all the ingredients (to make sure you have everything!) and the necessary equipment you will need to make the process flow more smoothly.

The butter, eggs, and milk should be at room temperature before you even think about beginning a recipe. And if you're making a cheesecake, it is especially important that the cream cheese be at room temperature. Most of the recipes in this book and most cookbooks call for "softened" butter, but it is important to recognize that softened butter is actually butter at room temperature. If you press your finger into properly softened butter, it will leave an indentation but will retain its shape. If the butter is very soft, it is difficult to achieve the desired texture and density in baked goods. When making icing or frosting, let your butter get a bit softer than if you were baking a dessert. If the eggs need to be separated for your recipe, it's easier to separate them when they're cold and then allow them to come to room temperature.

When selecting the pans you will use, keep in mind that metal pans should be smooth, because uneven or blackened pans tend to absorb heat unevenly. I prefer to use glass baking dishes for pies, brownies, and squares, and I strongly discourage using pans with a nonstick surface. You can grease the pans using a pastry brush or by rubbing in the butter or shortening with your fingers. Just make sure that, either way, the pan's surface is evenly and not overly coated. After greasing, sprinkle a few spoonfuls of flour into the pan, shake it around until the entire inside of the pan is coated with flour, and then empty out the excess flour by tapping the pan gently. When called for in the recipe, line the bottom of the pan with waxed paper. If you're making a cake, this is a foolproof way to prevent it from sticking to the pan.

Cakes

One of the most important tips that I can offer concerns the creaming of butter. When creaming butter, it is necessary to beat the butter until it is light and fluffy, which takes about three minutes depending on the type of mixer you're using. I have found that most people, especially if they're just learning to bake or if they don't bake very often, don't realize how long three minutes is, and so they wind up not creaming their butter for the proper amount of time. Creaming the butter properly ensures that the dessert (especially if it's a cake) will have the volume and texture desired. It is also important to add the sugar gradually, to beat continuously, and to keep beating for an additional two to three minutes. The eggs should then be added, one at a time, beating until the mixture is thick, fluffy, and pale in color. Up to this point it is almost impossible to beat the batter too much.

To make it easier to alternately add the ingredients, I suggest that you thoroughly combine (or sift, if called for) the dry ingredients in a bowl or a large measuring cup, and mix the milk, buttermilk, or other liquid together with the extract in a separate measuring cup. When adding the wet and dry ingredients, do so alternately, in three parts, beating after each addition. The ingredients should be blended thoroughly and the batter should be smooth, but be sure not to overbeat or the cake will lose its light texture. Remember to use a rubber spatula to scrape down the batter from the sides and the bottom of the bowl, making sure the ingredients are well blended throughout the mixing process.

When dividing the batter between the prepared pans, you can use a measuring cup if you like to ensure that you have an equal amount of batter in each pan, and your rubber spatula to spread the batter evenly.

It is best to bake cake layers in the center of the oven, placing the pans on the same rack if possible, but not touching.

Icing

Before icing, be sure that the cake layers are completely cool. Icing will not stick to a warm cake, and a warm cake becomes soggy if iced.

Be sure to brush any crumbs off the sides of the cake layers and place the layers top side up (pan side down) on a level surface. If any of the layers are uneven, you can slice off the top using a serrated knife.

I find that the best way to frost a layer cake is by frosting between the layers first and then frosting the top and sides of the cake. If you make sure to keep plenty of icing on your spatula, the whole frosting process will go more smoothly. Keep in mind that this is one of those things that gets easier with practice.

Cookies

First, I highly recommend investing in a small ice cream scoop to use instead of a spoon for measuring your cookies. The one that I use for all of my cookie recipes measures approximately 1 tablespoon in capacity. The ice cream scoop gives you even, rounded cookies that hold their shape well while baking and, obviously, makes all the cookies the same size. (Keep in mind that if you make the cookies much smaller or larger than 1 tablespoon, you must adjust the baking time accordingly.)

Second, if it's summertime and it's really hot, and your cookie dough seems too soft, put the dough in the fridge for fifteen to twenty minutes before scooping. If you bake cookies with dough that is too soft, your cookies will spread out too much during baking.

Third, for evenly browned cookies I recommend baking only one sheet of cookies at a time on the center rack of the oven.

Last, the most common problem people seem to have is that they wait too long to take the cookies out of the oven. Pay attention to the recommended baking time. The right time to take cookies out of the oven is when they look almost the way you'd like them to look but still slightly underdone. They may look a little underdone, but cookies continue to bake after they come out of the oven.

Pies

With just a little practice, a golden, flaky piecrust is not difficult to achieve. Not having anyone at my house to teach me when I was growing up, it took me a little while to learn how to make pies, too. Although conventional wisdom dictates the use of chilled shortening or butter, I have found that using unchilled vegetable shortening results in a dough that is very easy to handle and produces a consistently flaky texture. For my crusts I always use Crisco butter flavor shortening, which gives the butter flavor that I'm looking for but, again, keeps the flakiness that I love. (By the way, using Crisco sticks makes for really easy measuring.)

Most important, I really discourage using a food processor or standing mixer for making pies because it's so easy to overwork the dough when using these methods. Start out with the flour in a bowl, then add the shortening, cut into about half-inch pieces. Using a pastry blender, work in the shortening until the mixture resembles coarse crumbs (at this point the shortening should be pea-sized). Sprinkle the *ice cold* water, by tablespoons, over the flour mixture, stirring it in gently with a fork. Be sure not to overwork the dough. Shape the dough into a ball. (If you're making a double-crust pie, divide the dough into two disks, wrap one in waxed paper, and set aside.) Place your dough on a lightly floured piece of waxed paper, flatten the dough gently with the palm of your hand, and sprinkle the top lightly with flour. Using a lightly floured rolling pin, roll out the dough from the center evenly in all directions. If the dough sticks to the rolling pin, dust it lightly with more flour. Be careful to use only as much flour as is necessary to roll out the dough, keeping in mind that adding too much flour during the rolling-out process will produce a dry, tough crust. Lay your glass pie dish facedown on top of the circle of dough, flip the pan over, gently pressing the dough into the pan, and then remove the waxed paper.

Trim the dough, leaving a half inch around the edge. If you are making a single-crust pie, tuck the overhanging pastry dough underneath itself and crimp. If you are making a double-crust pie, add the filling, mounding it in the center. Then roll out the second disk, lift the waxed paper with the dough, flip it over the filling, and remove the waxed paper. Trim the edges of the dough and pinch together the top and bottom crusts.

Cheesecakes

The most frustrating thing about cheesecakes is the tendency for cracks to appear in the cake. The most important thing you can do to avoid these surface cracks is to not overwhip the cream cheese, because this can cause too much air to be incorporated into the batter. Be sure to set the mixer on the lowest speed and to beat the cream cheese until very smooth before adding the other ingredients. Then, when adding the other ingredients, mix only until well incorporated. Extremes in temperature can also lead to surface cracks. Avoid opening the oven door as much as possible while baking, and cool the cheesecake gradually in an oven that has been turned off.

The second most frustrating thing is not being quite sure when the cake is actually done. I make them all the time and still stand pondering in front of the oven, jiggling the pan, trying to make sure it's completely cooked yet still perfectly creamy. You can set the timer for an hour, but after that it's really practice and a good judgment call—there's just no fancy advice to give.

note: If you would like to make individual-size cheesecakes, as we do at the bakery, divide the cheesecake batter into twelve 3 x 3-inch cheesecake pans with removeable bottoms, and bake for 25 to 30 minutes, or until the edges are set and the center moves only slightly. The MagicLine individual cheesecake pans that we use are available at www.complementstothechef.com (or 1-800-895-CHEF).

A few last words . . .

Be sure to check that your oven temperature is correct, and if you're not sure, use an oven thermometer. Many ovens are off by twenty-five degrees or more, which of course significantly alters your baking time.

Be sure that the oven is preheated to the proper temperature so that your batter is not sitting in the pan or pans at room temperature, waiting to go into the oven. Once the leavening agent is mixed into the batter it is important to get it right into the oven to start baking.

The time to arrange the oven racks to the right level for whatever you're baking is BEFORE you preheat the oven—not when you're ready to bake your dessert. (Too much heat escapes while you're rearranging the racks if you wait to do it then.)

If it's the first time you're attempting a recipe and you are uncertain of the baking time, test the dessert several times toward the end of the recommended time.

If you do a lot of baking (or cooking) with nuts, like I do, it's a great time saver to toast the nuts in advance so that they're ready anytime you need them for a recipe. Often, if I have the oven on at 350 degrees for something I'm making, I'll take the opportunity to put in a pan of nuts to toast at the same time.

Always use large eggs for baking. It is important to realize that an egg is a liquid ingredient, and substituting extra-large or jumbo eggs will throw off the balance of a recipe.

Always use unsalted butter, not margarine or vegetable shortening (unless shortening is specifically called for in the recipe).

Always use pure vanilla extract, not imitation, which can taste tinny and artificial.

If you would like to make the breakfast buns, like we do them at the bakery, I recommend using a bun pan (which has straight sides) instead of a large muffin pan. Bun pans are available in two sizes from The Baker's Catalogue, at www.bakerscatalogue.com (or 1-800-827-6836).

Coffee Cakes, Quick Breads, and Breakfast Buns

Apple Cake with Cinnamon Sugar Topping

I love to get up really early when I have guests visiting for the weekend and make this coffee cake. Using canned sliced apples makes it extremely easy to prepare, and it's out of the oven before everyone else wakes up for breakfast.

2 cups all-purpose flour

2 teaspoons baking powder

1 teaspoon salt

²/₃ cup vegetable oil (preferably canola)

1 cup sugar

2 large eggs, at room temperature

1 cup milk

1 teaspoon vanilla extract

One 20-ounce can sliced apples, drained and patted dry

¹/₂ cup sugar mixed with 1 teaspoon cinnamon

Preheat oven to 325 degrees.

Grease and lightly flour a 10-inch tube pan.

In a small bowl, sift together the flour, baking powder, and salt. Set aside.

In a large bowl, on the medium speed of an electric mixer, beat together the oil, sugar, and eggs until light and thick, about 3 minutes. Add the dry ingredients in three parts, alternating with the milk and vanilla, beating after each addition until smooth. In a separate small bowl, toss the apples with half of the cinnamon-sugar mixture, then stir half of the apples into the batter. Pour the batter into the prepared pan. Drop the remaining apples on top of the batter and sprinkle with the remaining cinnamon sugar. Bake for 60–70 minutes, or until a cake tester inserted in the center of the cake comes out clean. Let the cake cool in the pan for 1 hour, then remove from the pan and cool completely on a wire rack.

MAKES ONE 10-INCH CAKE

Banana Bread with Coconut and Pecans

*H*onestly, I was never a big banana bread fan until the idea of adding coconut came to me one afternoon and inspired this recipe, which turned out wonderfully. It's surprisingly good with a little salted butter as well as plain.

3 cups flour

1 ½ teaspoons baking soda

¾ teaspoon cinnamon

¾ teaspoon salt

¾ cup canola oil

1 ½ cups sugar

3 large eggs, at room temperature, well beaten

1 ½ teaspoons vanilla extract

1 ½ cups mashed ripe bananas

¾ cup sour cream

1 ½ cups coarsely chopped toasted pecans (see Note)

¾ cup sweetened shredded coconut

*N*ote: To toast the pecans, place on a baking sheet in a 350-degree oven for 15 minutes, or until lightly browned and fragrant.

Preheat oven to 350 degrees.

Grease and lightly flour a 10-inch tube pan.

In a medium-size bowl, sift together the flour, baking soda, cinnamon, and salt. Set aside.

In a large bowl, on the medium speed of an electric mixer, beat together the oil and sugar. Add the eggs and vanilla, and beat well. Add the bananas and sour cream, and mix well. Add the dry ingredients and mix until just combined. Stir in the pecans and coconut. Pour the batter into the prepared pan. Bake for 60–70 minutes, or until a cake tester inserted into the center of the bread comes out with moist crumbs attached. Let cool for at least 1 hour before removing from the pan and serving.

MAKES ONE 10-INCH CAKE

Pear Streusel Breakfast Buns

$\mathcal{A}$ really nice, not-too-sweet breakfast treat. You can substitute apples for the pears if you like.

STREUSEL TOPPING

1 cup firmly packed light brown sugar

1 1/2 teaspoons cinnamon

4 tablespoons (1/2 stick) unsalted butter, softened and cut into small pieces

1 1/2 cups chopped walnuts

BUNS

1 1/2 cups all-purpose flour

1/4 teaspoon baking soda

1/4 teaspoon salt

3/4 cup (1 1/2 sticks) unsalted butter, softened

1 cup sugar

3 eggs, at room temperature

6 tablespoons milk

1 teaspoon vanilla extract

1 1/2 cups coarsely chopped peeled pears

Preheat oven to 350 degrees.

Grease and lightly flour 12 bun pans or large muffin cups.

To make the topping: In a medium-size bowl, combine the brown sugar and cinnamon. Using a pastry blender, cut in the butter until the mixture resembles coarse crumbs. Add the walnuts, and using your hands, toss until the ingredients are well combined. Set aside.

To make the buns: In a small bowl, combine the flour, baking soda, and salt. Set aside.

In a large bowl, on the medium speed of an electric mixer, cream the butter until smooth. Add the sugar gradually and beat until fluffy, about 3 minutes. Add the eggs, one at a time, beating well after each addition.

Add the dry ingredients in two parts, alternating with the milk and vanilla, beating until well incorporated. Stir in pears. Spoon the batter into the bun pans or muffin cups. Sprinkle the topping over the buns, being sure to keep the crumbs within the muffin cups (otherwise the buns are difficult to remove from the pan).

Bake for 20–25 minutes, or until a cake tester inserted in the center of the bun comes out clean.

MAKES 12 BUNS

Zucchini Walnut Bread

*T*his is a recipe that I've been making since I was a teenager, and I've tweaked it here and there over the years. If you have a vegetable garden and can pick your own fresh squash, it makes all the difference.

1 cup all-purpose flour
1 teaspoon baking soda
$\frac{1}{2}$ teaspoon baking powder
$\frac{1}{2}$ teaspoon salt
$\frac{1}{2}$ teaspoon cinnamon
$\frac{1}{2}$ cup vegetable oil (preferably canola)

$\frac{3}{4}$ cup sugar
2 large eggs, at room temperature
$\frac{1}{2}$ teaspoon vanilla extract
1 cup shredded zucchini (including skin)
$\frac{3}{4}$ cup chopped walnuts

Preheat oven to 350 degrees.

Grease and flour a 9 x 5 x 3-inch loaf pan.

In a small bowl, combine the flour, baking soda, baking powder, salt, and cinnamon. Set aside.

In a large bowl, on the medium speed of an electric mixer, beat together the oil, sugar, eggs, and vanilla until light and thick, about 3 minutes. Stir in the zucchini.

Add the dry ingredients and mix until just combined. Stir in the walnuts.

Pour the batter into the prepared pan. Place on a baking sheet and bake for 50–60 minutes, or until a cake tester inserted in the center of the loaf comes out with moist crumbs attached. Let cool for at least 1 hour before serving.

MAKES 1 LOAF

Blueberry Coffee Cake with Vanilla Glaze

*T*his light and moist coffee cake is simple to prepare and makes a good addition to breakfast or brunch.

CAKE
2 cups all-purpose flour
2 teaspoons baking powder
1 teaspoon salt
$2/3$ cup vegetable oil (preferably canola)
1 cup sugar
2 large eggs, at room temperature

1 cup milk
1 teaspoon vanilla extract
$1\frac{1}{2}$ cups fresh blueberries, lightly coated with flour

VANILLA GLAZE
$1\frac{1}{4}$ cups confectioners' sugar, sifted
$\frac{1}{2}$ cup heavy cream
$\frac{1}{2}$ teaspoon vanilla extract

Preheat oven to 325 degrees.

Grease and lightly flour a 10-inch tube pan.

In a small bowl, sift together the flour, baking powder, and salt. Set aside.

In a large bowl, on the medium speed of an electric mixer, beat together the oil, sugar, and eggs until light and thick, about 3 minutes. Add the dry ingredients in three parts, alternating with the milk and vanilla, beating after each addition until smooth. Fold in the blueberries. Pour the batter into the prepared pan and bake for 60–70 minutes, or until a cake tester inserted in the center of the cake comes out clean. Let the cake cool in the pan for 1 hour. Remove from the pan and cool completely on a wire rack.

To make the vanilla glaze: In the top of a double boiler, over barely simmering water, combine the sugar, cream, and vanilla. Stir until the ingredients are well blended, about 2 minutes. Pour into a glass measuring cup and cover until ready to use. When the cake is completely cool, drizzle the glaze decoratively over the cake. Allow the glaze to set for 1 hour before slicing and serving the cake.

MAKES ONE 10-INCH CAKE

Cream Cheese Crumb Buns

*T*his recipe was inspired, believe it or not, by the Freihoffer-brand crumb cheese coffee cake. A few years back, some of the staff were at my house (when I first moved and didn't yet have a kitchen), and we were eating the Freihoffer cake (right out of the box, of course) and said, "This is really good. We could make this at the bakery." So we came up with this recipe.

CREAM CHEESE FILLING
½ pound (one 8-ounce package) cream cheese, softened
3 tablespoons unsalted butter, softened
2 tablespoons sugar
1 large egg yolk, at room temperature
½ teaspoon vanilla extract

CRUMB TOPPING
1½ cups all-purpose flour
1 cup firmly packed light brown sugar
2 teaspoons baking powder
½ cup (1 stick) unsalted butter, softened and cut into small pieces

BUNS
1½ cups all-purpose flour
1 teaspoon baking powder
¼ teaspoon salt
½ cup solid vegetable shortening
½ cup sugar
2 large eggs, at room temperature
½ cup milk

Preheat oven to 350 degrees.

Grease and lightly flour 16 bun pans or large muffin cups.

To make the filling: In a medium-size bowl, beat the cream cheese and butter until smooth and creamy. Add the sugar, egg yolk, and vanilla, and beat well. Set aside.

To make the topping: In a large bowl, mix together the flour, sugar, and baking powder. Using a pastry blender, cut in the butter until the mixture resembles coarse crumbs. Set aside.

To make the buns: In a small bowl, combine the flour, baking powder, and salt. Set aside.

In a large bowl, on the medium speed of an electric mixer, beat together the shortening and sugar until smooth. Add the eggs, one at a time, beating well after each addition. Add the dry ingredients, in two parts, alternating with the milk and beating until well incorporated. Spoon the batter into the bun pans or muffin cups. Bake for 10 minutes.

Remove from the oven, and working quickly but carefully, place a tablespoon of the cream cheese filling in the center of each bun and press it down gently with the back of the spoon. Sprinkle the crumb topping over the cream cheese, covering the entire top of the bun and being sure to keep the crumbs within the muffin cups (otherwise the buns are difficult to remove from the pan). Return to the oven and bake for an additional 13 minutes. (Do not use a cake tester to check for doneness—it will only come out with cream cheese filling attached!)

Allow to cool for 30 minutes before serving. These are best when eaten warm with the filling still a little gooey.

MAKES 16 BUNS

Brown Sugar
Pecan Cake

I love cake that is not too sweet or too fancy and can be eaten at the kitchen table in the afternoon with tea or coffee. This can also be served with whipped cream if you like.

2 cups cake flour (not self-rising)
2 teaspoons baking powder
$\frac{1}{2}$ teaspoon salt
$\frac{3}{4}$ cup (1$\frac{1}{2}$ sticks) unsalted butter, softened
1$\frac{1}{2}$ cups firmly packed light brown sugar

2 large eggs, at room temperature
1 cup milk
1 teaspoon vanilla extract
1$\frac{1}{2}$ cups chopped toasted pecans (see Note)

Note: To toast the pecans, place on a baking sheet in a 350-degree oven for 15 minutes, or until lightly browned and fragrant.

Preheat oven to 325 degrees.

Grease and lightly flour a 10-inch tube pan.

In a small bowl, sift together the flour, baking powder, and salt. Set aside.

In a large bowl, on the medium speed of an electric mixer, cream the butter until smooth. Add the sugar gradually and beat until fluffy, about 3 minutes. Add the eggs, one at a time, beating well after each addition. Add the dry ingredients in three parts, alternating with the milk and vanilla, beating after each addition until smooth. Stir in 1$\frac{1}{4}$ cups (reserving $\frac{1}{4}$ cup) of the pecans. Pour the batter into the prepared pan and sprinkle the remaining $\frac{1}{4}$ cup of pecans over the top.

Bake for 60–70 minutes, or until a cake tester inserted in the center of the cake comes out clean. Let the cake cool in the pan for 1 hour. Remove from the pan and cool completely on a wire rack.

MAKES ONE 10-INCH CAKE

Raspberry Cream Cheese Breakfast Buns

These buns have been our most popular breakfast item at the bakery since the first day we opened our doors. The flavors of the cream cheese and the preserves work really well together.

BUN
1¾ cups all-purpose flour
1 teaspoon baking powder
½ teaspoon baking soda
¼ teaspoon salt
½ pound (one 8-ounce package) cream cheese, softened
½ cup (1 stick) unsalted butter, softened
1 cup sugar
2 large eggs, at room temperature
¼ cup milk
½ teaspoon vanilla extract

TOPPING
½ cup raspberry preserves

GARNISH
Confectioners' sugar

Preheat oven to 350 degrees.

Grease and lightly flour 9 bun pans or large muffin cups.

In a small bowl, combine the flour, baking powder, baking soda, and salt. Set aside.

In a large bowl, on the medium speed of an electric mixer, beat together the cream cheese, butter, and sugar until smooth, about 3 minutes. Add the eggs and beat well. Add the dry ingredients in two parts, alternating with the milk and vanilla. Spoon the batter into the bun pans or muffin cups, filling them about two-thirds full. Drop 3 small dollops (about a teaspoonful each) of raspberry preserves onto the top of each bun and, using the tip of a sharp knife, swirl the preserves into the batter, forming a decorative pattern. Bake for 25–30 minutes, or until a cake tester inserted in the center of the bun comes out clean.

Allow the buns to cool for about 30 minutes before sprinkling with confectioners' sugar and serving.

MAKES 9 BUNS

Cookies

Chocolate Chocolate Chip Drop Cookies

*A*n old-fashioned, chewy chocolate cookie with little extra bursts of chocolate from the miniature chips.

1 cup all-purpose flour
6 tablespoons unsweetened Dutch process cocoa
1/2 teaspoon baking powder
1/4 teaspoon salt
5 tablespoons unsalted butter, softened
5 tablespoons solid vegetable shortening

1 cup sugar plus 1 tablespoon (for sprinkling)
1 large egg, at room temperature
1 teaspoon vanilla extract
1/2 cup miniature semisweet chocolate chips

In a small bowl, combine the flour, cocoa, baking powder, and salt. Set aside.

In a large bowl, cream the butter, shortening, and sugar until smooth, about 3 minutes. Add the egg and vanilla, and beat well. Add the dry ingredients and mix thoroughly. Stir in the chocolate chips. Drop by rounded teaspoonfuls onto ungreased cookie sheets, leaving several inches between for expansion. Sprinkle lightly with the sugar. Place the cookie sheets in the refrigerator and chill for 20 minutes.

Preheat oven to 350 degrees.

Bake for 10–12 minutes. Cool the cookies on the sheets for 5 minutes and then remove to a wire rack to cool completely.

MAKES 2 DOZEN COOKIES

Iced Ginger Cookies

I've been making these cookies for years now, and I still get really excited every autumn when I bake the first batch of the season. They're chewy and spicy with just the right amount of sweet icing. (My boyfriend, Tadhg, insists that I mention he prefers them without the icing.)

COOKIE

2 cups all-purpose flour

2 teaspoons baking soda

1 teaspoon ginger

1 teaspoon cinnamon

$1/2$ teaspoon salt

$3/4$ cup vegetable oil (preferably canola)

1 cup sugar plus 1 tablespoon (for sprinkling)

1 large egg, at room temperature

$1/4$ cup light unsulphured molasses

ICING

$1/2$ cup confectioners' sugar, sifted

1 tablespoon solid vegetable shortening

2 teaspoons water

Preheat oven to 350 degrees.

In a small bowl, combine the flour, baking soda, ginger, cinnamon, and salt. Set aside.

In a large bowl, on the medium speed of an electric mixer, beat together the oil and sugar for 2–3 minutes. Add the egg and molasses, and beat well. Add the dry ingredients and mix thoroughly. Drop by rounded teaspoonfuls onto ungreased cookie sheets, leaving several inches between for expansion. Sprinkle lightly with sugar. Bake for 12 minutes. Cool the cookies on the sheets for 5 minutes, and then remove to a wire rack to cool completely.

To make the icing: Combine the sugar, shortening, and water, and beat until smooth and creamy. Cover until ready to use.

When the cookies are completely cool, spread a very thin layer of icing on each cookie with a small knife or spatula. Let the icing set before stacking the cookies or they will stick together.

MAKES 2½ DOZEN COOKIES

Coconut Oatmeal Drop Cookies

I'm always striving to make the perfect crispy but chewy oatmeal cookie. I'm not fond of raisins, so I add coconut instead for extra texture and sweetness.

1 1/2 cups all-purpose flour
1 teaspoon baking soda
1 teaspoon cinnamon
1/4 teaspoon salt
1 cup (2 sticks) unsalted butter, softened
1 cup firmly packed light brown sugar

1/2 cup granulated sugar
1 large egg, at room temperature
1 1/2 teaspoons vanilla extract
1 1/2 cups rolled oats (not quick-cooking)
1 cup sweetened shredded coconut

Preheat oven to 375 degrees.

In a small bowl, combine the flour, baking soda, cinnamon, and salt. Set aside.

In a large bowl, cream the butter with the sugars until smooth, about 2 minutes. Add the egg and vanilla, and beat well. Add the dry ingredients and mix thoroughly. Stir in the oats and coconut. Drop by rounded teaspoonfuls onto ungreased cookie sheets, leaving several inches between for expansion. Bake for 12–14 minutes, or until lightly golden.

Cool the cookies on the sheets for 5 minutes, and then remove to a wire rack to cool completely.

MAKES 3 1/2 DOZEN COOKIES

Snickerdoodles

This soft cinnamon-sugar cookie has been around for ages, and I don't think anyone knows where the name comes from. When I was growing up, we always made these at Christmastime, so we still do that at the bakery.

2½ cups all-purpose flour
2 teaspoons cream of tartar
1 teaspoon baking soda
¼ teaspoon salt
1 cup (2 sticks) unsalted butter, softened
1½ cups sugar

2 large eggs, at room temperature
2 tablespoons milk
1 teaspoon vanilla extract

6 tablespoons sugar mixed with 2 teaspoons cinnamon, for sprinkling

In a small bowl, combine the flour, cream of tartar, baking soda, and salt. Set aside.

In a large bowl, cream the butter and sugar until smooth, about 2 minutes. Add the eggs, milk, and vanilla, and beat well. Add the dry ingredients and mix thoroughly. Wrap the dough tightly with plastic wrap and chill in the refrigerator for 2 hours.

Preheat oven to 350 degrees.

Drop by rounded teaspoonfuls onto ungreased cookie sheets, leaving several inches between for expansion. (I recommend leaving extra room between these cookies because they spread more than most.) Sprinkle generously with the cinnamon-sugar mixture. Bake for 12–14 minutes.

Cool the cookies on the sheets for 5 minutes, and then remove to a wire rack to cool completely.

MAKES 3 DOZEN COOKIES

White Chocolate Pecan Drop Cookies

*T*wo of my favorite ingredients—toasted pecans and creamy white chocolate—together in what is definitely the most often baked cookie at our house.

1 ½ cups all-purpose flour
1 teaspoon baking soda
½ teaspoon salt
⅔ cup (1 ⅓ sticks) unsalted butter, softened
½ cup granulated sugar
½ cup firmly packed light brown sugar

1 large egg, at room temperature
1 teaspoon vanilla extract
1 cup coarsely chopped toasted pecans (see Note)
⅔ cup coarsely chopped white chocolate (preferably Lindt)

Note: To toast the pecans, place on a baking sheet in a 350-degree oven for 15 minutes, or until lightly browned and fragrant.

Preheat oven to 350 degrees.

In a small bowl, combine the flour, baking soda, and salt. Set aside.

In a large bowl, cream the butter with the sugars until smooth, about two minutes. Add the egg and vanilla, and beat well. Add the dry ingredients and mix thoroughly. Stir in the pecans and white chocolate. Drop by rounded teaspoonfuls onto ungreased cookie sheets, leaving several inches between for expansion. Bake for 10–12 minutes, or until lightly golden.

Cool the cookies on the sheets for 5 minutes, and then remove to a wire rack to cool completely.

MAKES 3 DOZEN COOKIES

Raspberry Hazelnut Linzer Cookies

*A*nother big Christmastime favorite at the bakery, these cookies require a few steps but are really not difficult to make and are quite festive.

3 cups all-purpose flour
$1/4$ teaspoon salt
$1^{1}/_2$ cups (3 sticks) unsalted butter, softened
1 cup granulated sugar
$1^{1}/_2$ teaspoons vanilla extract

1 cup finely chopped (not ground) toasted hazelnuts (see Note)
$1/3$ cup raspberry preserves
$1/2$ cup confectioners' sugar (for dredging)

Note: To toast the hazelnuts, place on a baking sheet in a 350-degree oven for 15 minutes, or until lightly browned and fragrant.

In a small bowl, combine the flour and salt. Set aside.

In a large bowl, cream the butter and sugar until smooth, about two minutes. Add the vanilla and beat well. Add the dry ingredients in three parts, adding the nuts with the last portion, and mix until just combined. Shape the dough into two flat disks, wrap each disk tightly with plastic wrap, and refrigerate for 30 minutes.

Working with one disk at a time, roll out the dough on a lightly floured surface to $1/4$-inch thickness. Using a 3-inch fluted cutter, cut out the cookies and place them on baking sheets lined with waxed paper. Place the baking sheets in the refrigerator and chill for an additional 15 minutes.

Preheat oven to 350 degrees.

Remove the baking sheets from the refrigerator, and using a $1/2$-inch fluted cutter, cut a circle out of the center of half of the cookies. Arrange on ungreased baking sheets, 2 inches apart, and bake for 15–18 minutes, or until lightly golden around the edges.

Cool the cookies on the sheets for 5 minutes, and then remove to a wire rack to cool completely.

Spread 1 teaspoon of preserves on the flat side of the cookies without the cutout centers. Sandwich the cutout cookies with the cookies spread with the preserves. Dredge the cookies on both sides with the confectioners' sugar.

MAKES 20 COOKIES

Toffee Pecan Drop Cookies

*I*f you can't find the toffee pieces in your supermarket's baking section, you can substitute chopped Heath bar candy—but I love these cookies without any chocolate in them.

2 cups all-purpose flour	1 large egg, at room temperature
1 teaspoon baking soda	1 ½ teaspoons vanilla extract
½ teaspoon salt	1 ½ cups coarsely chopped toasted
1 cup (2 sticks) butter	pecans (see Note)
¾ cup firmly packed light brown sugar	1 cup toffee pieces
¼ cup granulated sugar	

Note: To toast the pecans, place on a baking sheet in a 350-degree oven for 15 minutes, or until lightly browned and fragrant.

Preheat oven to 350 degrees.

In a small bowl, combine the flour, baking soda, and salt. Set aside.

In a large bowl, cream the butter with the sugars until smooth, about 2 minutes. Add the egg and vanilla, and beat well. Add the dry ingredients and mix thoroughly. Stir in the pecans and toffee. Drop by rounded teaspoonfuls onto ungreased cookie sheets, leaving several inches between for expansion. Bake for 10–12 minutes, or until lightly golden.

Cool the cookies on the sheets for 5 minutes, and then remove to a wire rack to cool completely.

MAKES 4 DOZEN COOKIES

Oatmeal Peanut Butter Chip Cookies

After countless evenings of standing in front of the open refrigerator, dipping freshly baked oatmeal cookies into the jar of Skippy . . .

1 cup all-purpose flour
1/2 teaspoon baking soda
1/2 teaspoon salt
1/4 teaspoon cinnamon
3/4 cup (1 1/2 sticks) unsalted butter, softened
3/4 cup firmly packed light brown sugar

1/2 cup granulated sugar
1 large egg, at room temperature
1 1/2 teaspoons vanilla extract
2 1/2 cups quick-cooking oats (not regular, old-fashioned rolled oats)
1 cup peanut butter chips

Preheat oven to 350 degrees.

In a small bowl, combine the flour, baking soda, salt, and cinnamon. Set aside.

In a large bowl, cream the butter with the sugars until smooth, about 2 minutes. Add the egg and vanilla, and beat well. Add the dry ingredients and mix thoroughly. Stir in the oats and peanut butter chips. Drop by rounded teaspoonfuls onto ungreased cookie sheets, leaving several inches between for expansion. Bake for 11–13 minutes.

Cool the cookies on the sheets for 5 minutes, and then remove to a wire rack to cool completely.

MAKES 3 DOZEN COOKIES

Pumpkin Walnut Cookies with Brown Butter Frosting

*T*his spicy, cakelike cookie comes from Nancy Sinko, the mother of Barbara and Shelly, who have worked with me at the bakery since the very beginning. Nancy frosts these cookies with a cream cheese icing—either way, they're really good.

Cookie
2½ cups all-purpose flour
1 tablespoon baking powder
1 teaspoon salt
1 teaspoon allspice
½ teaspoon cinnamon
¼ teaspoon ginger
4 tablespoons (½ stick) unsalted
    butter, softened
1½ cups firmly packed light brown
    sugar
2 large eggs, at room temperature

1 cup canned pumpkin puree
2 teaspoons vanilla extract
1 cup chopped walnuts

Frosting
2 cups confectioners' sugar
3 tablespoons milk
1 teaspoon vanilla extract
3 tablespoons unsalted butter

Garnish
Walnut halves

Preheat oven to 375 degrees.

To make the cookies: In a small bowl, combine the flour, baking powder, salt, all-spice, cinnamon, and ginger. Set aside.

In a large bowl, cream the butter and sugar until evenly combined. Add the eggs, pumpkin, and vanilla, and beat well. Add the dry ingredients and mix thoroughly. Stir in the walnuts. Drop by rounded teaspoonfuls onto ungreased cookie sheets, leaving several inches between for expansion. The batter will seem extremely soft compared with most cookie doughs, but it will firm up during baking. Bake for 12 minutes. Cool the cookies on the sheets for 10–12 minutes, and then remove to a wire rack to cool completely.

To make the frosting: Place the sugar, milk, and vanilla in a small bowl. Set aside. In a small saucepan over medium-high heat, cook the butter until lightly browned, about 3–5 minutes. Remove from the heat, add to the other ingredients, and beat until smooth and creamy. Cover until ready to use.

When the cookies are completely cool, spread a generous amount of frosting on each cookie, and top with a walnut half. Let the icing set before stacking the cookies or they will stick together.

Peanut Butter Chocolate Chip Pecan Cookies

*F*or those of you who, like me, can't resist adding peanut butter to desserts, this is basically a chocolate chip cookie with peanut butter chips as well. Also, the milk in the batter gives these cookies a lovely texture.

2½ cups all-purpose flour
1 teaspoon baking soda
½ teaspoon salt
1 cup (2 sticks) unsalted butter, softened
1 cup firmly packed light brown sugar
⅓ cup granulated sugar

1 large egg, at room temperature
2 tablespoons milk
1½ teaspoons vanilla extract
1½ cups coarsely chopped toasted pecans (see Note)
1 cup peanut butter chips
½ cup semisweet chocolate chips

Note: To toast the pecans, place on a baking sheet in a 350-degree oven for 15 minutes, or until lightly browned and fragrant.

Preheat oven to 350 degrees.

In a small bowl, combine the flour, baking soda, and salt. Set aside.

In a large bowl, cream the butter with the sugars until smooth, about 2 minutes. Add the egg, milk, and vanilla, and beat well. Add the dry ingredients and mix thoroughly. Stir in the pecans, peanut butter chips, and chocolate chips. Drop by rounded teaspoonfuls onto ungreased cookie sheets, leaving several inches between for expansion. Bake for 10–12 minutes, or until lightly golden.

Cool the cookies on the sheets for 5 minutes, and then remove to a wire rack to cool completely.

MAKES 5 DOZEN COOKIES

Brownies
and
Bar Cookies

White Chocolate Pecan Bars

*T*his bar cookie has a really nice brown sugar shortbread base with a topping of white chocolate and pecans.

BAR

2 cups all-purpose flour

1/2 teaspoon salt

1 cup (2 sticks) unsalted butter, softened

1 cup firmly packed light brown sugar

1 large egg, at room temperature

1 teaspoon vanilla extract

1/2 cup coarsely chopped toasted pecans (see Note)

TOPPING

1 1/2 cups coarsely chopped white chocolate

1/2 cup coarsely chopped toasted pecans (see Note)

Note: To toast the pecans, place on a baking sheet in a 350-degree oven for 15 minutes, or until lightly browned and fragrant.

Preheat oven to 350 degrees.

Grease and lightly flour a 13 x 9-inch baking pan.

In a small bowl, combine the flour and salt. Set aside.

In a large bowl, beat together the butter, sugar, egg, and vanilla until creamy, about 2–3 minutes. Add the dry ingredients and mix thoroughly. Stir in the pecans. Spread the batter evenly in the prepared pan. Bake for 25 minutes.

Remove from the oven and immediately sprinkle the white chocolate on top. Let stand for 5 minutes and then gently spread the melted chocolate in a thin layer over the bars. Sprinkle with the pecans.

Allow to cool to room temperature (the white chocolate should harden) or overnight before cutting and serving.

MAKES TWENTY-FOUR 2-INCH BARS

Apple Bars with Oatmeal Crumb Topping

A perfect autumn treat—all the flavors of apple pie, but unlike the more fragile pie, these bars are easily wrapped up for lunches and picnics.

CRUST
1 cup (2 sticks) unsalted butter, softened and cut into small pieces
2 cups all-purpose flour

TOPPING
1 ½ cups all-purpose flour
1 cup firmly packed light brown sugar
⅔ cup rolled oats (not quick cooking) plus 3 tablespoons (for sprinkling)

½ teaspoon cinnamon
⅔ cup (1 ⅓ sticks) unsalted butter, softened and cut into small pieces

FILLING
One 21-ounce can apple pie filling

GLAZE
1 cup confectioners' sugar, sifted
1 tablespoon plus 1 teaspoon water

Preheat oven to 350 degrees.

To make the crust: In a large bowl, on the medium speed of an electric mixer, beat together the butter and flour until crumbly and well combined. Transfer the mixture to an ungreased 13 x 9-inch baking pan and, using your hands, pat the crust firmly and evenly into the pan. Bake for 20 minutes. Remove from the oven and allow to cool completely, about 45 minutes.

To make the topping: In a large bowl, mix together the flour, sugar, oats, and cinnamon. Using a pastry blender, cut in the butter until the mixture resembles coarse crumbs. Then, using your hands, toss until all the ingredients are well combined. Set aside.

When the crust is cool, gently and evenly spread the apple filling over the crust, leaving a ¼-inch edge all around. Sprinkle the crumb topping over the filling, then sprinkle the additional 3 tablespoons of rolled oats over the crumb topping. Bake for 45 minutes. Allow to cool to room temperature.

To make the glaze: Combine the sugar and water, and beat until smooth. Cover until ready to use. When the bars are completely cool, drizzle the glaze decoratively over the crumb topping. Allow the glaze to set for 15–20 minutes before cutting and serving.

MAKES TWENTY-FOUR 2-INCH BARS

Blondies with Cream Cheese Swirl and Pecans

There have been lots of recipes over the years for cream cheese swirl brownies, but never the blondie and cream cheese combination, which seemed perfect to me. If, like me, you are not a huge chocolate fan, you'll love these.

CREAM CHEESE FILLING
4 ounces (one-half of an 8-ounce package) cream cheese (not softened)
2 tablespoons sugar
1 large egg yolk, at room temperature
1 tablespoon all-purpose flour

BLONDIES
1 ½ cups cake flour (not self-rising)
1 teaspoon baking powder

¼ teaspoon salt
¾ cup (1 ½ sticks) unsalted butter, softened
1 ¼ cups firmly packed light brown sugar
¼ cup granulated sugar
2 large eggs, at room temperature
2 teaspoons vanilla extract
½ cup coarsely chopped toasted pecans (see Note)

Note: To toast the pecans, place on a baking sheet in a 350-degree oven for 15 minutes, or until lightly browned and fragrant.

Preheat oven to 350 degrees.

Grease and lightly flour a 13 x 9-inch baking pan.

To make the cream cheese filling: In a medium-size bowl, beat the cream cheese and sugar until smooth. Add the egg yolk and flour, and beat well. Set aside.

To make the blondies: In a small bowl, combine the flour, baking powder, and salt. Set aside. In a large bowl, cream the butter with the sugars until smooth, about 2 minutes. Add the eggs and vanilla, and beat well. Add the dry ingredients and mix thoroughly. Spread the batter evenly in the prepared pan.

Drop the cream cheese mixture by teaspoonfuls over the batter. Using a small knife, swirl the cream cheese into the batter, forming a decorative pattern. Sprinkle the pecans evenly over the batter.

Bake for 35–40 minutes, or until a cake tester inserted in the center of the pan comes out with moist crumbs attached. Do not overbake. Allow to cool to room temperature or overnight before cutting and serving.

MAKES TWENTY-FOUR 2-INCH BLONDIES

Walnut Brown Sugar Squares

This is, hands down, the quickest and easiest recipe in this book. You don't even need to wait for the butter to soften because there's no butter (or any shortening) in it!

½ cup plus 2 tablespoons all-purpose
   flour
¼ teaspoon baking soda
¼ teaspoon salt

1 cup firmly packed light brown sugar
1 large egg, at room temperature
1 teaspoon vanilla extract
1 cup chopped walnuts

Preheat oven to 350 degrees.

Lightly grease an 8 x 8-inch baking pan.

In a small bowl, combine the flour, baking soda, and salt. Set aside.

In a medium-size bowl, on the medium speed of an electric mixer, beat together the sugar, egg, and vanilla until creamy and smooth, about 2 minutes. Add the dry ingredients and mix thoroughly. Stir in the walnuts, reserving 2 tablespoons. Transfer the batter to the prepared pan and, using your hands, spread the batter evenly. Sprinkle with the remaining 2 tablespoons of walnuts. Bake for 25 minutes. The center will not be set but do not overbake.

Cool to room temperature, cover tightly with plastic wrap, and allow to set overnight before cutting and serving.

MAKES SIXTEEN 2-INCH SQUARES

Chocolate Fudge Brownies with Butterscotch Chips and Pecans

*T*hese are really dense, really fudgy brownies. I've always loved the combination of butterscotch and chocolate.

½ cup all-purpose flour
⅛ teaspoon salt
4 tablespoons (½ stick) unsalted
  butter
8 ounces semisweet chocolate
2 ounces unsweetened chocolate

2 large eggs, at room temperature
1 cup sugar
2 teaspoons vanilla extract
1 cup coarsely chopped toasted
  pecans (see Note)
⅓ cup butterscotch chips

Note: To toast the pecans, place on a baking sheet in a 350-degree oven for 15 minutes, or until lightly browned and fragrant.

Preheat oven to 325 degrees.

Grease and lightly flour an 8 x 8-inch baking pan.

In a small bowl, combine the flour and salt. Set aside.

In a medium-size saucepan over low heat, melt the butter with the chocolates, stirring occasionally until smooth. Remove from the heat and allow to cool to lukewarm, 5–10 minutes.

Meanwhile, beat the eggs with the sugar until light and creamy, 2–3 minutes. Add the vanilla and beat well. Add the chocolate mixture and beat until well combined. Add the dry ingredients and mix thoroughly. Stir in half of the pecans and half of the butterscotch chips. Spread the batter evenly in the prepared pan. Bake for 20 minutes. Remove from the oven and sprinkle the remaining pecans and butterscotch chips evenly over the brownie batter. Return to the oven and bake for an additional 15–20 minutes, or until a cake tester inserted in the center of the pan comes out with moist crumbs attached. Do not overbake.

Allow to cool to room temperature or overnight before cutting and serving.

MAKES SIXTEEN 2-INCH BROWNIES

Apricot Cream Cheese Streusel Bars

*T*his delicate bar combines a creamy filling with apricot preserves and a sweet crumb topping.

CRUST
1 cup (2 sticks) unsalted butter,
softened and cut into small pieces
2 cups all-purpose flour

CREAM CHEESE FILLING
1/2 pound (one 8-ounce package)
cream cheese (not softened)
1/3 cup sugar
1 large egg, at room temperature

1 teaspoon vanilla extract

STREUSEL TOPPING
1 1/2 cups all-purpose flour
1 1/2 cups confectioners' sugar
3/4 cup (1 1/2 sticks) unsalted butter,
softened and cut into small pieces

APRICOT FILLING
3/4 cup apricot preserves (preferably
unsweetened)

Preheat oven to 350 degrees.

To make the crust: In a large bowl, on the medium speed of an electric mixer, beat together the butter and flour until crumbly and well combined. Transfer the mixture to an ungreased 13 x 9-inch baking pan and, using your hands, pat the crust firmly and evenly into the pan. Bake for 15 minutes. Remove from the oven and allow to cool completely, about 45 minutes.

To make the cream cheese filling: In a medium-size bowl, on the medium speed of an electric mixer, beat together the cream cheese and sugar until smooth and creamy. Add the egg and vanilla, and continue to beat until well combined. Set aside.

To make the streusel topping: In a medium-size bowl, mix together the flour and sugar. Using a pastry blender, cut in the butter until the mixture resembles coarse crumbs. Then, using your hands, toss until the ingredients are well combined. Set aside.

When the crust is cool, spread the cream cheese filling evenly over the crust, leaving a ¼-inch edge all around. Gently spread a thin layer of apricot filling over the cream cheese. Sprinkle the streusel topping over the entire top. Bake for 35 minutes. Cool to room temperature, cover tightly with plastic wrap, and allow to set overnight before cutting and serving.

MAKES TWENTY-FOUR 2-INCH BARS

Coconut Pecan Shortbread Squares

This bar cookie has a simple shortbread crust and layers of pecans and coconut. It couldn't be easier to make—or more delicious.

CRUST

1 cup (2 sticks) unsalted butter, softened and cut into small pieces
2 cups all-purpose flour

TOPPING

2 cups coarsely chopped toasted pecans (see Note)
1 cup sweetened shredded coconut
One 14-ounce can sweetened condensed milk

Note: To toast the pecans, place on a baking sheet in a 350-degree oven for 15 minutes, or until lightly browned and fragrant.

Preheat oven to 350 degrees.

To make the crust: In a large bowl, on the medium speed of an electric mixer, beat together the butter and flour until crumbly and well combined. Transfer the mixture to an ungreased 13 x 9-inch baking pan and, using your hands, pat the crust firmly and evenly into the pan. Bake for 15 minutes. Remove from the oven and allow to cool for 30 minutes.

Sprinkle the pecans and then the coconut over the crust. Pour the can of sweetened condensed milk on top to completely cover the coconut. Use a spatula to spread it if necessary. Bake for 30–35 minutes, or until lightly golden.

Cool to room temperature, cover tightly with plastic wrap, and allow to set overnight before cutting and serving.

MAKES TWENTY-FOUR 2-INCH SQUARES

Hello Dolly Bars

*A*fter years of hearing customers and friends from the South tell me about a bar cookie that was just like the Magic Cookie Bar we serve at the bakery, I finally have received an actual recipe for Hello Dolly Bars from Maria Howard of Peculiar, Missouri. It turns out that the ingredients are a little different, and they're even easier to make—you just dump all the ingredients in a bowl and mix.

2 cups graham cracker crumbs
2 cups coarsely chopped pecans
2 cups sweetened shredded coconut
1 cup semisweet chocolate chips
1 cup butterscotch chips

¾ cup (1 ½ sticks) unsalted butter, melted
One and a half 14-ounce cans sweetened condensed milk

Preheat oven to 325 degrees.

Lightly grease a 13 x 9-inch baking pan.

Mix together all the ingredients except the sweetened condensed milk in a large bowl. Transfer the mixture to the prepared pan and pat down evenly with your hands. Pour the sweetened condensed milk over the top to cover, using a spatula to spread if necessary. Bake for 30–35 minutes, or until lightly golden. Cool to room temperature, cover tightly with plastic wrap, and allow to set overnight before cutting and serving.

MAKES TWENTY-FOUR 2-INCH BARS

Chocolate Brownies with Caramel, Peanut Butter, and Pecans

*T*his is a variation on a brownie that we've been serving at the bakery for years. In this version, though, the caramel and pecans, plus the surprisingly tasty addition of peanut butter chips, are layered between the graham cracker crust and the brownie.

CRUST
2¼ cups graham cracker crumbs
¾ cup (1½ sticks) unsalted butter, melted

CARAMEL FILLING
1 pound vanilla caramels
¼ cup heavy cream
¾ cup coarsely chopped toasted pecans (see Note)
½ cup peanut butter chips

BROWNIE
½ cup all-purpose flour
¾ teaspoon baking powder
½ teaspoon salt
½ cup (1 stick) unsalted butter
6 ounces unsweetened chocolate
1½ cups sugar
3 large eggs, at room temperature
1 teaspoon vanilla extract

Note: To toast the pecans, place on a baking sheet in a 350-degree oven for 15 minutes, or until lightly browned and fragrant.

Preheat oven to 350 degrees.

To make the crust: In a medium-size bowl, combine the graham cracker crumbs and melted butter. Press firmly into an ungreased 13 x 9-inch baking pan. Set aside.

To make the caramel filling: In a medium-size saucepan over low heat, melt the caramels with the cream, stirring occasionally, until smooth. Remove from the heat and pour over the graham cracker crust. Use a spatula to spread it evenly. Sprinkle the pecans and peanut butter chips over the caramel. Set aside.

To make the brownie: In a small bowl, combine the flour, baking powder, and salt. Set aside. In a medium-size saucepan over low heat, melt the butter and chocolate, stirring occasionally until smooth. Remove from the heat, transfer to a large bowl, and allow the mixture to cool for 5 minutes. Add the sugar, eggs, and vanilla, and beat well. Add the dry ingredients and mix thoroughly. Pour the batter over the pecans and peanut butter chips to completely cover the caramel layer. Bake for 35–45 minutes, or until a cake tester inserted in the center of the pan comes out with moist crumbs attached. Do not overbake.

Cool to room temperature, cover tightly with plastic wrap, and allow to set overnight before cutting and serving.

MAKES TWENTY-FOUR 2-INCH BROWNIES

Shelly's Cherry Squares

*T*his recipe comes from Shelly Sinko, who has been baking at Magnolia longer than anyone else. It's based on a cookie that her mom made when she was growing up.

½ cup (1 stick) unsalted butter, softened	1 teaspoon vanilla extract
1½ cups granulated sugar	2 cups all-purpose flour
4 large eggs, at room temperature	½ cup canned cherry pie filling
	Confectioners' sugar for sprinkling

Preheat oven to 350 degrees.

Grease and lightly flour a 13 x 9-inch baking pan.

In a large bowl, on the medium speed of an electric mixer, cream the butter with the granulated sugar until smooth, about 2 minutes. Add the eggs, one at a time, beating well after each addition. Add the vanilla. Add the flour and mix thoroughly.

Spread the dough evenly in the prepared pan. With a small, sharp knife, score into twenty-four 2-inch squares.

Place a teaspoon of cherry pie filling (each containing one cherry) on each scored square. Bake for 30–35 minutes, or until a cake tester inserted in the center of the pan comes out clean.

Allow to cool to room temperature, then sprinkle generously with confectioners' sugar before cutting and serving.

MAKES TWENTY-FOUR 2-INCH SQUARES

Blondies with White and Dark Chocolate Chunks

A moist and chewy butterscotch bar with two kinds of chocolate and lots of walnuts.

1 1/2 cups cake flour (not self-rising)
1 teaspoon baking powder
1/4 teaspoon salt
3/4 cup (1 1/2 sticks) unsalted butter, softened
1 cup firmly packed light brown sugar
1/2 cup granulated sugar

2 large eggs, at room temperature
2 teaspoons vanilla extract
1 cup coarsely chopped walnuts
3/4 cup coarsely chopped white chocolate
1/2 cup coarsely chopped semisweet chocolate

Preheat oven to 350 degrees.

Grease and lightly flour a 13 x 9-inch baking pan.

In a small bowl, combine the flour, baking powder, and salt. Set aside.

In a large bowl, cream the butter with the sugars until smooth, about 2 minutes. Add the eggs and vanilla, and beat well. Add the dry ingredients and mix thoroughly. Stir in the walnuts and chocolate chunks. Spread the batter evenly in the prepared pan. Bake for 35–40 minutes, or until a cake tester inserted in the center of the pan comes out with moist crumbs attached. Do not overbake.

Allow to cool to room temperature or overnight before cutting and serving.

MAKES TWENTY-FOUR 2-INCH BLONDIES

Pumpkin Bars
with Cream Cheese Icing

We start making these bars at the bakery the week of Halloween. And every year both the customers and the staff can hardly wait that long. They're very, very good.

Bars
1 ½ cups all-purpose flour
1 ½ teaspoons baking powder
1 ½ teaspoons cinnamon
1 teaspoon baking soda
¼ teaspoon salt
1 ¼ cups canned pumpkin puree
1 ¼ cups sugar
¾ cup vegetable oil (preferably canola)

3 large eggs, at room temperature
½ cup coarsely chopped toasted pecans (see Note)

Icing
½ recipe Cream Cheese Icing (page 118)

Garnish
½ cup coarsely chopped toasted pecans (see Note)

Note: To toast the pecans, place on a baking sheet in a 350-degree oven for 15 minutes, or until lightly browned and fragrant.

Preheat oven to 350 degrees.

Grease and lightly flour a 13 x 9-inch baking pan.

To make the bars: In a small bowl, sift together the flour, baking powder, cinnamon, baking soda, and salt. Set aside.

In a large bowl, on the medium speed of an electric mixer, beat together the pumpkin, sugar, oil, and eggs until smooth, about 3 minutes. Add the dry ingredients and mix thoroughly. Stir in the pecans. Pour the batter into the prepared pan. Bake for 25–30 minutes, or until a cake tester inserted in the center of the pan comes out clean.

Remove from the oven and allow to cool completely before icing the top with the cream cheese icing. Garnish with pecans as desired.

MAKES TWELVE 3-INCH BARS

Pies and Tarts

Apple Tart with Hazelnut Brown Sugar Topping

*T*his tart is a nice alternative to apple pie, and it makes a great dessert for a dinner party, especially if served with vanilla ice cream and perhaps some caramel sauce.

BROWN SUGAR TOPPING
3/4 cup all-purpose flour
1/2 cup firmly packed light brown sugar
6 tablespoons unsalted butter,
    softened and cut into small pieces
1/2 cup coarsely chopped hazelnuts

FILLING
3 cups thinly sliced tart apples
1/3 cup sugar
1 tablespoon flour

1 teaspoon vanilla extract

CRUST
6 tablespoons unsalted butter,
    softened
2 tablespoons sugar
1 large egg, at room temperature
1 large egg yolk, at room temperature
1 1/2 cups all-purpose flour
1 tablespoon baking powder

Preheat oven to 325 degrees.

To make the topping: In a medium-size bowl, mix together the flour and sugar. Using a pastry blender, cut in the butter until the mixture resembles coarse crumbs. Add the hazelnuts and, using your hands, toss until all the ingredients are well combined. Set aside.

To make the filling: Place all the ingredients in a large bowl and toss gently until the fruit is evenly coated. Set aside.

To make the crust: In a large bowl, on the low speed of an electric mixer, cream the butter and sugar until smooth. Add the egg and egg yolk, and mix well. Add the flour and baking powder, and beat until just combined. Gather the dough into a ball and on a lightly floured surface, roll it out to fit a 10-inch tart pan. Fit the dough into the pan and trim the edge flush with the rim of the pan.

Transfer the fruit filling into the crust and sprinkle the brown sugar topping evenly over the fruit. Place the tart on a baking sheet and bake for 50 minutes.

Cool on a wire rack for 1–2 hours. Serve warm or at room temperature.

MAKES ONE 10-INCH TART

Strawberry Double-Crust Pie

$\mathcal{A}$ few summers ago I was searching for a good strawberry pie recipe and realized that all the recipes I could find called for a prebaked pie shell, a filling made on top of the stove, and then a chilling period in the refrigerator. I really wanted to make a regular double-crusted, bake-in-the-oven strawberry pie—and with the right amount of tapioca to balance the juiciness of the berries, you can.

FILLING

5 cups fresh strawberries, sliced in half

½ cup sugar

¼ cup quick-cooking minute tapioca

1 teaspoon vanilla extract

CRUST

2⅓ cups all-purpose flour

1 cup solid vegetable shortening, cut into small pieces

6 tablespoons ice water

GLAZE

1 tablespoon milk

1 tablespoon sugar

Preheat oven to 400 degrees.

To make the filling: Place all the ingredients in a large bowl and toss gently until the fruit is evenly coated. Let stand for 15 minutes while preparing the crust.

To make the crust: Place the flour in a large bowl and, using a pastry blender, cut in the shortening until the pieces are pea-size. Sprinkle the ice water by tablespoonfuls over the flour mixture and toss with a fork until all the dough is moistened. Gather the dough into a ball, separate into two pieces, and wrap one piece in waxed paper and set aside. Roll out the first piece on a lightly floured surface to fit a 9-inch glass pie dish and trim, leaving ½ inch around the edge.

Transfer the fruit filling into the bottom crust. Unwrap the reserved piece of dough, roll it out as the top crust, and trim to fit. Fold the ½-inch excess on the bottom crust over the top edge. Seal by crimping the edges together. Brush the top crust with the milk, then sprinkle evenly with the sugar. Make several 1-inch steam slits in the center of the pie with the tip of a paring knife. Place the pie on a baking sheet, lower the oven temperature to 350 degrees, and bake for 60–70 minutes, until the crust is golden.

Cool on a wire rack for at least 2 hours. Serve warm or at room temperature, with sweetened whipped cream, if desired.

MAKES ONE 9-INCH PIE

Nancy's Prize-winning Blueberry Pie

*T*his recipe comes from Nancy Schatz of Augusta, Maine. The pie won first prize in the 1991 Old Hallowell Day bake-off.

CRUST
2½ cups all-purpose flour

3 tablespoons sugar

1 teaspoon salt

4 tablespoons (½ stick) unsalted butter, chilled and cut into small pieces

3 tablespoons solid vegetable shortening, chilled and cut into small pieces

5 tablespoons orange juice (use a variety without pulp)

FILLING
3 cups fresh blueberries

1 cup sugar

3 tablespoons quick-cooking minute tapioca

3 tablespoons brandy

2 tablespoons freshly squeezed lemon juice

¼ teaspoon cinnamon

2 tablespoons unsalted butter, chilled and cut into small pieces

To make the crust: Place the flour, sugar, and salt in a large bowl. Using a pastry blender, cut in the butter and shortening until the pieces are pea-size. Sprinkle the orange juice by tablespoonfuls over the flour mixture and toss with a fork until all the dough is moistened. Gather the dough into a ball and separate into two pieces. Wrap the pieces tightly with plastic wrap and refrigerate for 30 minutes. Five minutes before removing the chilled pie dough from the refrigerator, prepare your filling.

To make the filling: In a large bowl, place the berries, sugar, tapioca, brandy, lemon juice, and cinnamon. Toss gently until the fruit is evenly coated. Let stand for 15 minutes while rolling out the crust.

Preheat oven to 425 degrees.

On a lightly floured surface, roll out half of the dough to fit a 9-inch glass pie dish and trim, leaving ½ inch around the edge. Transfer the fruit filling into the bottom crust, mounding it in the center. Dot with the butter.

Roll out the top crust and trim it to fit, folding the ½-inch excess on the bottom crust over the top edge. Seal by crimping the edges together. Make several 1-inch steam slits in the center of the pie with the tip of a paring knife. Place the pie on a baking sheet and bake for 15 minutes. Lower the oven temperature to 350 degrees and continue baking for an additional 30 minutes.

Cool on a wire rack for at least 2 hours before serving.

MAKES ONE 9-INCH PIE

Chocolate Pecan Pudding Pie

I have this wonderful childhood memory of a pie that had a custardy chocolate filling with pecans that wasn't like the standard chocolate pecan pie, which I usually find too rich and sweet. This recipe combines our chocolate pudding from the bakery with pecans and a pastry crust—a simple old-fashioned dessert that comes pretty close to my memory.

CRUST
1 cup plus 2 tablespoons all-purpose flour
½ cup solid vegetable shortening
3 tablespoons ice water

FILLING
1 cup sugar
6 tablespoons unsweetened cocoa (do not use Dutch process!)
¼ cup cornstarch
Pinch of salt
3 cups milk
1½ cups coarsely chopped toasted pecans (see Note)
1 tablespoon vanilla extract

GARNISH
Sweetened whipped cream
Coarsely chopped toasted pecans

Note: To toast the pecans, place on a baking sheet in a 350-degree oven for 15 minutes, or until lightly browned and fragrant.

Preheat oven to 425 degrees.

To make the crust: Place the flour in a large bowl and, using a pastry blender, cut in the shortening until the pieces are pea-size. Sprinkle the ice water by tablespoonfuls over the flour mixture and toss with a fork until all the dough is moistened. Gather the dough into a ball and roll out on a lightly floured surface to fit a 9-inch glass pie dish and trim, leaving ½ inch around the edge. Fold the edges under all around the rim and crimp. Prick all over the bottom and sides of the crust with a fork. Place the crust on a baking sheet and bake for 20–25 minutes or until the edges are lightly golden. Remove from the oven and allow to cool to room temperature, about 45 minutes.

To make the filling: In a medium-size saucepan, combine the sugar, cocoa, cornstarch, and salt. Add the milk and whisk over medium heat until the pudding thickens and begins to bubble, about 15 minutes. Remove from the heat and stir in the pecans and vanilla. Pour immediately into the cooled crust. Cover the top of the pie with waxed paper to prevent a skin from forming and cool for 30 minutes.

Remove the waxed paper, cover the pie tightly with plastic wrap, and refrigerate for at least 3 hours or overnight. Serve with sweetened whipped cream, and then garnish with the pecans.

MAKES ONE 9-INCH PIE

Nectarine
Double-Crust Pie

*N*o one ever seems to make nectarine pie, and I'm not sure why. I adore nectarines (possibly even more than peaches), and this is one of my favorite summertime desserts to make when nectarines are perfectly ripe and in season.

FILLING
5 cups sliced ripe nectarines (see
    Note)
½ cup granulated sugar
¼ cup firmly packed light brown sugar
¼ cup quick-cooking minute tapioca
1 teaspoon vanilla extract

CRUST
2⅓ cups all-purpose flour
1 cup solid vegetable shortening, cut
    into small pieces
6 tablespoons ice water

GLAZE
1 tablespoon milk
1 tablespoon sugar

Note: Be sure to blanch the nectarines in boiling water for 60 seconds, transfer to an ice water bath, and remove the skins before slicing.

Preheat oven to 400 degrees.

To make the filling: Place all the ingredients in a large bowl and toss gently until the fruit is evenly coated. Let stand for 15 minutes while preparing the crust.

To make the crust: Place the flour in a large bowl and, using a pastry blender, cut in the shortening until the pieces are pea-size. Sprinkle the ice water by tablespoonfuls over the flour mixture and toss with a fork until all the dough is moistened. Gather the dough into a ball, separate into two pieces. Wrap one piece in waxed paper and set aside. Roll out the first piece on a lightly floured surface to fit a 9-inch glass pie dish and trim, leaving ½ inch around the edge.

Transfer the fruit filling into the bottom crust. Unwrap the reserved piece of dough, roll it out as the top crust, and trim to fit. Fold the ½-inch excess on the bottom crust over the top edge. Seal by crimping the edges together. Brush the top crust with the milk, then sprinkle evenly with the sugar. Make several 1-inch steam slits in the center of the pie with the tip of a paring knife. Place the pie on a baking sheet, lower the oven temperature to 350 degrees, and bake for 60–70 minutes, until the crust is golden.

Cool on a wire rack for at least 2 hours. Serve warm or at room temperature with sweetened whipped cream, if desired.

MAKES ONE 9-INCH PIE

Plum Tart with Almond Streusel Topping

I had never really given much thought to baking with plums until my friend Kate had us over for dinner one evening and served a plum galette for dessert. I went right out to the market, got some plums, and started experimenting. Be sure to use ripe, flavorful plums for this tart.

STREUSEL TOPPING
¾ cup all-purpose flour
¾ cup sugar
6 tablespoons unsalted butter,
    softened and cut into small pieces
½ cup chopped toasted almonds (see
    Note)

FILLING
3 cups thinly sliced plums
¼ cup sugar

1 tablespoon flour
1 teaspoon vanilla extract

CRUST
6 tablespoons unsalted butter,
    softened
2 tablespoons sugar
1 large egg, at room temperature
1 large egg yolk, at room temperature
1½ cups all-purpose flour
1 tablespoon baking powder

Note: To toast the almonds, place on a baking sheet in a 350-degree oven for 15 minutes, or until lightly browned and fragrant.

Preheat oven to 325 degrees.

To make the topping: In a medium-size bowl, mix together the flour and sugar. Using a pastry blender, cut in the butter until the mixture resembles coarse crumbs. Add the almonds and, using your hands, toss until all the ingredients are well combined. Set aside.

To make the filling: Place all the ingredients in a large bowl and toss gently until the fruit is evenly coated. Set aside.

To make the crust: In a large bowl, on the low speed of an electric mixer, cream the butter and sugar until smooth. Add the egg and egg yolk, and mix well. Add the flour and baking powder, and beat until just combined. Gather the dough into a ball and roll it out on a lightly floured surface to fit a 10-inch tart pan. Fit the dough into the pan and trim the edge flush with the rim of the pan.

Transfer the fruit filling into the crust and sprinkle the streusel topping evenly over the fruit. Place the tart on a baking sheet and bake for 45 minutes.

Cool on a wire rack for 1–2 hours. Serve warm or at room temperature with sweetened whipped cream, if desired.

MAKES ONE 10-INCH TART

Jill's Apple Pie

This is my friend Jill Rowe's favorite apple pie recipe. It was the most popular dessert that she made when she owned and ran a local restaurant, The Kitchen, near my home in upstate New York.

CRUST

2 cups all-purpose flour
1/2 teaspoon salt
2/3 cup solid vegetable shortening, chilled and cut into small pieces
4 tablespoons (1/2 stick) unsalted butter, chilled and cut into small pieces
5 tablespoons ice water

FILLING

3/4 cup sugar
2 tablespoons all-purpose flour
1/2 teaspoon cinnamon
1/8 teaspoon nutmeg
1/8 teaspoon salt
6 cups sliced tart green apples (preferably Granny Smith)
4 tablespoons (1/2 stick) unsalted butter, chilled and cut into small pieces

To make the crust: Place the flour and salt in a large bowl and, using a pastry blender, cut in the shortening and butter until the pieces are pea-size. Sprinkle the ice water by tablespoonfuls over the flour mixture and toss with a fork until all the dough is moistened. Gather the dough into a ball and separate into two pieces. Wrap the pieces tightly with plastic wrap and refrigerate for 30 minutes.

Preheat oven to 400 degrees.

To make the filling: Place the sugar, flour, cinnamon, nutmeg, and salt in a large bowl. Add the apples and toss gently until the fruit is evenly coated.

Roll out one piece of the dough on a lightly floured surface to fit a 9-inch glass pie dish and trim, leaving 1/2 inch around the edge. Transfer the fruit filling into the bottom crust, mounding it in the center. Dot with the butter.

Roll out the second piece of dough into a top crust and trim to fit. Fold the 1/2-inch excess on the bottom crust over the top edge. Seal by crimping the edges together.

Make several 1-inch steam slits in the center of the pie with the tip of a paring knife. Place the pie on a baking sheet and bake for 50 minutes.

Cool on a wire rack for at least 2 hours. Serve warm or at room temperature with sweetened whipped cream, if desired.

MAKES ONE 9-INCH PIE

Pumpkin Pie

I think we all have our favorite pumpkin pie recipe. This is my latest version—not too spicy and with a hint of bourbon.

CRUST

1 cup plus 2 tablespoons all-purpose
  flour
½ cup solid vegetable shortening
3 tablespoons ice water

FILLING

One 15-ounce can pumpkin puree
2 large eggs, at room temperature

½ cup granulated sugar
¼ cup firmly packed light brown sugar
1 teaspoon cinnamon
½ teaspoon allspice
¼ teaspoon salt
1 ¼ cups evaporated milk
3 tablespoons bourbon

Preheat oven to 425 degrees.

To make the crust: Place the flour in a large bowl and, using a pastry blender, cut in the shortening until the pieces are pea-size. Sprinkle the ice water by tablespoonfuls over the flour mixture and toss with a fork until all the dough is moistened. Gather the dough into a ball, roll out on a lightly floured surface to fit a 9-inch glass pie dish and trim, leaving ½ inch around the edge. Fold the edges under all around the rim and crimp. Set aside.

To make the filling: In a large bowl, on the medium speed of an electric mixer, combine the pumpkin and eggs, and beat well. Add the sugars, cinnamon, allspice, and salt, and mix until well combined. Combine the evaporated milk and bourbon, and stir into the pumpkin mixture in three parts.

Pour the filling into the prepared crust. Place the pie on a baking sheet and bake for 15 minutes. Lower the oven temperature to 350 degrees and continue baking for an additional 50–60 minutes, or until a tester inserted in the center of the pie comes out clean.

Cool on a wire rack for at least 2 hours. Serve warm or at room temperature with sweetened whipped cream, if desired.

MAKES ONE 9-INCH PIE

Cheese Pies
and
Cheesecakes

Strawberry Cream Cheese Pie with Graham Cracker Crust

*A*t the farmers market near my house every summer, there is a woman who grows and sells the most perfect half-wild strawberries I have ever eaten. The first pint of the season we eat straight out of the container, and with the second pint I make this really great cream cheese pie.

CRUST
1/2 cup (1 stick) unsalted butter, melted
1 1/4 cups graham cracker crumbs
1/2 cup chopped toasted pecans (see Note)
1/4 cup unpacked light brown sugar

FILLING
1 pound (two 8-ounce packages) cream cheese, softened
1 cup confectioners' sugar
1/4 cup sour cream
1 teaspoon vanilla extract

TOPPING
1 pint (2 cups) fresh strawberries, sliced in half

Note: To toast the pecans, place on a baking sheet in a 350-degree oven for 15 minutes, or until lightly browned and fragrant.

Preheat oven to 350 degrees.

To make the crust: In a medium-size bowl, combine the butter with the graham cracker crumbs, pecans, and sugar. Press firmly into a lightly buttered 9-inch glass pie dish. Place on a baking sheet and bake for 12 minutes. Remove from the oven and allow to cool on a wire rack.

To make the filling: In a large bowl, on the low speed of an electric mixer, beat together the cream cheese and sugar until smooth and creamy. Add the sour cream and vanilla, and continue to beat at low speed until well combined.

Refrigerate the filling while the crust is cooling. When the crust is completely cooled, spread the filling evenly in the crust with a rubber spatula. Arrange the sliced strawberries on top of the filling in a decorative manner.

Refrigerate the pie for at least 8 hours or overnight to ensure that the filling sets.

MAKES ONE 9-INCH PIE

Caramel Apple Pecan Cheesecake

*E*very Thanksgiving at my cousin Polly's house we gather the evening before to do the holiday baking, and every year I am called upon to create a new cheesecake. This is last year's recipe, and it was loved by all.

CRUST
1 cup cake flour (not self-rising)
¼ cup firmly packed light brown sugar
½ cup (1 stick) unsalted butter, softened and cut into small pieces
1 cup chopped toasted pecans (see Note)

FILLING
2 pounds (four 8-ounce packages) cream cheese, softened
1¼ cups sugar
5 large eggs, at room temperature
2 tablespoons heavy cream

1 tablespoon vanilla extract

APPLE TOPPING
2½ cups thinly sliced tart apples (such as Granny Smith)
¼ cup sugar
⅛ teaspoon cinnamon
1 tablespoon unsalted butter

GARNISH
⅔ cup Caramel Sauce (page 124)
⅓ cup coarsely chopped toasted pecans (see Note)

Note: To toast the pecans, place on a baking sheet in a 350-degree oven for 15 minutes, or until lightly browned and fragrant.

Preheat oven to 350 degrees.

To make the crust: In a large bowl, mix together the flour and sugar. Using a pastry blender, cut in the butter until the mixture resembles coarse crumbs. Add the pecans and, using your hands, toss until all the ingredients are well combined. Press into the bottom of a buttered 10-inch springform pan. Bake for 20 minutes.

Remove from the oven and allow to cool on a wire rack. Lower the oven temperature to 325 degrees.

To make the filling: In a large bowl, on the low speed of an electric mixer, beat the cream cheese until very smooth. Gradually add the sugar. Add the eggs, one at a time. To ensure that the batter has no lumps and that no ingredients are stuck to the bottom of the bowl, stop the mixer several times and scrape down the sides of the bowl with a rubber spatula. Stir in the heavy cream and vanilla.

Pour the batter into the prepared pan and set the pan on a baking sheet. Bake until the edges are set and the center moves only slightly when the pan is shaken, about 1 hour. At the end of the baking time, turn off the heat and, using a wooden spoon to keep the oven door slightly ajar, cool the cake in the oven for 1 hour before removing. Cover and refrigerate for at least 12 hours or overnight.

To make the apple topping: Toss the apples with the sugar and cinnamon. In a medium-size saucepan, melt the butter over medium-high heat. Add the apples and cook, stirring occasionally, until the apples are very soft and easily pierced with a fork, 8–10 minutes. Remove the apples from the heat, transfer them to a small bowl, and allow to cool to room temperature, about 45 minutes. When the apples have cooled, spread them evenly in a thin layer over the top of the cheesecake. Return the cake to the refrigerator.

Remove the cake from the refrigerator 15–30 minutes before cutting and serving. To garnish, drizzle the caramel decoratively over the apples and then sprinkle with the pecans.

MAKES ONE 10-INCH CHEESECAKE

Cream Cheese Pecan Pie

*T*his is one of my favorite new pie recipes. The surprising combination of the cream cheese filling with the standard pecan pie filling is quite delicious.

CREAM CHEESE FILLING
$\frac{1}{2}$ pound (one 8-ounce package) cream cheese (not softened)
$\frac{1}{3}$ cup sugar
1 large egg, at room temperature
1 teaspoon vanilla extract
$\frac{1}{4}$ teaspoon salt

CORN SYRUP FILLING
3 large eggs, at room temperature
1 cup light corn syrup

$\frac{1}{4}$ cup firmly packed light brown sugar
1 teaspoon vanilla extract

CRUST
1 cup plus 2 tablespoons all-purpose flour
$\frac{1}{2}$ cup solid vegetable shortening
3 tablespoons ice water

$1\frac{1}{4}$ cups coarsely chopped toasted pecans (see Note)

Note: To toast the pecans, place on a baking sheet in a 350-degree oven for 15 minutes, or until lightly browned and fragrant.

Preheat oven to 375 degrees.

To make the cream cheese filling: In a medium-size bowl, on the medium speed of an electric mixer, beat together the cream cheese and sugar until smooth and creamy. Add the egg, vanilla, and salt, continuing to beat until ingredients are well blended and mixture is considerably thicker, 3–5 minutes. (I recommend using the whisk attachment if your mixer has one.) Set aside.

To make the corn syrup filling: In a small bowl, on the medium speed of an electric mixer, beat the eggs for 1 minute. Add the corn syrup, sugar, and vanilla, and beat 1 minute more. Set aside.

To make the crust: Place the flour in a large bowl and, using a pastry blender, cut in the shortening until the pieces are pea-size. Sprinkle the ice water by tablespoonfuls over the flour mixture and toss with a fork until all the dough is moistened. Gather the dough into a ball and roll it out on a lightly floured surface to fit a 9-inch glass pie dish and trim, leaving ½ inch around the edge. Fold the edges under all around the rim and crimp.

Spread the cream cheese filling evenly in the bottom of the crust. Sprinkle with the pecans. Slowly and carefully pour the corn syrup filling over the pecans. Place the pie on a baking sheet and bake for 50–60 minutes, or until the center of the pie is set.

Cool on a wire rack for at least 4 hours before cutting and serving. This pie is best served at room temperature, not warm, with sweetened whipped cream.

MAKES ONE 9-INCH PIE

Pumpkin Cheesecake
with Gingersnap Pecan Crust

*T*his cheesecake has been a huge success at the bakery since its introduction. It is a lovely dessert for an autumn dinner party. I love to make cheesecakes when I'm entertaining because they can be made one to two days in advance, before the guests even arrive.

CRUST
½ cup (1 stick) unsalted butter, melted
1½ cups gingersnap cookie crumbs
½ cup chopped toasted pecans (see Note)

FILLING
¾ pound (one and a half 8-ounce packages) cream cheese, softened
¾ cup granulated sugar

¾ cup firmly packed brown sugar
5 large eggs, at room temperature
1½ cups canned pumpkin puree
¾ cup heavy cream
1½ teaspoons cinnamon

GARNISH
Sweet Vanilla Whipped Cream (see page 121)
Toasted pecan halves (see Note)

Note: To toast the pecans, place on a baking sheet in a 350-degree oven for 15 minutes, or until lightly browned and fragrant.

Preheat oven to 325 degrees.

To make the crust: In a small bowl, combine the butter with the gingersnap cookie crumbs and pecans. Press into the bottom of a buttered 10-inch springform pan. Bake for 10 minutes. Remove from the oven and allow to cool on a wire rack.

To make the filling: In a large bowl, on the low speed of an electric mixer, beat the cream cheese until very smooth. Gradually add the sugars. Add the eggs, one at a time. Add the pumpkin puree and mix until just blended. To ensure that the batter has no lumps and that no ingredients are stuck to the bottom of the bowl, stop the mixer several times and scrape down the sides of the bowl with a rubber spatula. Stir in the heavy cream and cinnamon.

Pour the batter into the prepared pan and set the pan on a baking sheet. Bake until the edges are set and the center moves only slightly when the pan is shaken, about 1 hour. At the end of the baking time, turn off the heat and, using a wooden spoon to keep the oven door slightly ajar, cool the cake in the oven for 1 hour before removing. Cover and refrigerate for at least 12 hours or overnight.

Remove the cake from the refrigerator 15–30 minutes before cutting and serving. Garnish with the sweetened whipped cream and toasted pecan halves.

MAKES ONE 10-INCH CHEESECAKE

Peaches and Cream Pie
with Sugar Cookie Crust

This is a lovely, light summertime dessert that you should make only when you have peaches that are perfectly ripe and sweet.

CRUST

½ cup (1 stick) unsalted butter, softened
3 tablespoons sugar
1 large egg yolk, at room temperature
3 tablespoons heavy cream
1 ½ cups all-purpose flour
¼ teaspoon salt

FILLING

1 pound (two 8-ounce packages) cream cheese, softened
1 ½ cups confectioners' sugar
½ cup heavy cream
2 teaspoons vanilla extract

TOPPING

2 ½ cups thinly sliced ripe peaches (see Note)

Note: Be sure to blanch the peaches in boiling water for 60 seconds, transfer to an ice water bath, and remove the skins before slicing.

Preheat oven to 375 degrees.

To make the crust: In a large bowl, on the low speed of an electric mixer, cream the butter and sugar until smooth. Add the egg yolk and cream, and mix well. Add the flour and salt, and beat until just combined. Gather the dough into a ball and roll it out on a lightly floured surface to fit into a 9-inch glass pie dish. Fold the edges under all around the rim and crimp. Prick the bottom and sides all over with the tines of a fork. Cover the edge of the pie crust with aluminum foil, place on a baking sheet, and bake for 10 minutes. Carefully remove the foil and continue baking 20 minutes more, until the crust is crisp and golden. Remove from the oven and allow to cool on a wire rack.

To make the filling: In a large bowl, on the low speed of an electric mixer, beat together the cream cheese and sugar until smooth and creamy. Add the heavy cream and vanilla, and continue to beat at low speed until well combined.

Refrigerate the filling while the crust is cooling. When the crust is completely cooled, spread the filling evenly in the crust with a rubber spatula. Arrange the sliced peaches on top of the filling in a decorative manner.

Refrigerate the pie for at least 8 hours or overnight to ensure that the filling sets.

MAKES ONE 9-INCH PIE

Coconut Pecan Cheesecake

*T*his year's Thanksgiving cheesecake recipe . . .

CRUST
½ cup (1 stick) unsalted butter, melted
1¼ cups graham cracker crumbs
½ cup chopped toasted pecans (see Note)
¼ cup sugar

FILLING
2 pounds (four 8-ounce packages) cream cheese, softened
1 cup sugar

5 large eggs, at room temperature
1½ cups lightly packed sweetened shredded coconut
2 tablespoons heavy cream
2 teaspoons vanilla extract
1 teaspoon coconut extract

GARNISH
½ cup sweetened shredded coconut
¼ cup chopped toasted pecans (see Note)

Note: To toast the pecans, place on a baking sheet in a 350-degree oven for 15 minutes, or until lightly browned and fragrant.

Preheat oven to 325 degrees.

To make the crust: In a small bowl, combine the butter with the graham cracker crumbs, pecans, and sugar. Press into the bottom of a buttered 10-inch springform pan. Bake for 10 minutes. Remove from the oven and allow to cool on a wire rack.

To make the filling: In a large bowl, on the low speed of an electric mixer, beat the cream cheese until very smooth. Gradually add the sugar. Add the eggs, one at a time. To ensure that the batter has no lumps and that no ingredients are stuck to the bottom of the bowl, stop the mixer several times and scrape down the sides of the bowl with a rubber spatula. Stir in the coconut, heavy cream, and vanilla and coconut extracts.

(cont.)

$\mathcal{M}$agnolia's Vanilla and Chocolate Cupcakes
with Vanilla Buttercream

Red Velvet Cake with Creamy Vanilla Frosting

Pumpkin Cheesecake with Gingersnap Pecan Crust

$\mathcal{R}$aspberry Cream Cheese Breakfast Buns,
Nectarine Double-Crust Pie,
Vanilla Cake with Vanilla Buttercream,
Chocolate Cake with Vanilla Buttercream

Vanilla Sandwich Creme Cookie Ice Cream,
White Chocolate Peanut Brittle Ice Cream,
Old-Fashioned Chocolate Chip Ice Cream

*A*pple Tart with Hazelnut Brown Sugar Topping

IN THE JARS: Coconut Oatmeal Drop Cookies, Chocolate Chocolate Chip Drop Cookies, Peanut Butter Chocolate Chip Pecan Cookies

ON THE CAKE STAND: Iced Ginger Cookies, White Chocolate Pecan Drop Cookies, Blondies with Cream Cheese Swirl and Pecans

ON THE PLATE: Coconut Pecan Shortbread Squares, Chocolate Fudge Brownies with Butterscotch Chips and Pecans, White Chocolate Pecan Drop Cookies

$\mathcal{D}$evil's Food Cake with Seven-Minute Icing and Coconut

Pour the batter into the prepared pan and set the pan on a baking sheet. Bake until the edges are set and the center moves only slightly when the pan is shaken, about 1 hour. At the end of the baking time, turn off the heat and, using a wooden spoon to keep the oven door slightly ajar, cool the cake in the oven for 1 hour before removing. Cover and refrigerate for at least 12 hours or overnight.

Remove the cake from the refrigerator 15–30 minutes before cutting and serving. To garnish, sprinkle the additional coconut and pecans around the top edge of the cake.

MAKES ONE 10-INCH CHEESECAKE

Cupcakes and Layer Cakes

Black Bottom Cupcakes

*D*uring my quest in the kitchen for the perfect version of one of my favorite childhood treats, I was surprised to discover that many of my friends and neighbors (that is, testers) had never tried a black bottom cupcake before. If you're part of this group, you need to bake a batch—they're absolutely wonderful.

CREAM CHEESE FILLING
¾ pound (one and a half 8-ounce packages) cream cheese (not softened)
½ cup sugar
1 large egg, at room temperature
⅓ cup miniature semisweet chocolate chips

CUPCAKES
1¾ cups all-purpose flour
¾ cup unsweetened Dutch process cocoa
1 teaspoon baking soda
¼ teaspoon salt
½ cup vegetable oil (preferably canola)
1 cup sugar
1 cup buttermilk
2 teaspoons vanilla extract

Preheat oven to 350 degrees.

Line two 12-cup muffin tins with 18 cupcake papers.

To make the cream cheese filling: In a medium-size bowl, beat the cream cheese and sugar until smooth. Add the egg and beat well. Stir in the chocolate chips. Set aside.

To make the cupcakes: In a small bowl, combine the flour, cocoa, baking soda, and salt. Set aside. In a large bowl, on the medium speed of an electric mixer, beat together the oil and sugar. Add the dry ingredients in two parts, alternating with the buttermilk and vanilla, and making sure all ingredients are well blended.

Carefully spoon the cupcake batter into the cupcake liners, filling them about two-thirds full. Drop a small scoop (about 1½ tablespoons) of the cream cheese filling on top of each cupcake. Bake for 30–35 minutes, or until a cake tester inserted in the center of the cupcake comes out clean.

Cool the cupcakes in the tins for 30 minutes. Remove from the tins and cool completely on a wire rack.

MAKES 1½ DOZEN CUPCAKES

Strawberry Shortcake

*H*ere is an old-fashioned favorite that doesn't seem to go out of style. I recommend serving this cake relatively soon after assembling it, since the whipped cream tends to melt a little in the warm weather. I never refrigerate cakes because they dry out quickly when chilled.

CAKE
1½ cups self-rising flour
1¼ cups all-purpose flour
1 cup (2 sticks) unsalted butter, softened
2 cups sugar
4 large eggs, at room temperature
1 cup milk
1 teaspoon vanilla extract

CREAM FILLING
2 cups heavy cream
¼ cup confectioners' sugar
2 teaspoons vanilla extract

BERRY FILLING
2 pints (4 cups) ripe strawberries, sliced in half
2 tablespoons sugar

Preheat oven to 350 degrees.

Grease and lightly flour three 9 x 2-inch round cake pans, then line the bottoms with waxed paper.

To make the cake: In a small bowl, combine the flours and set aside. In a large bowl, on the medium speed of an electric mixer, cream the butter until smooth. Add the sugar gradually and beat until fluffy, about 3 minutes. Add the eggs, one at a time, beating well after each addition. Add the dry ingredients in three parts, alternating with the milk and vanilla. With each addition, beat until the ingredients are incorporated, but do not overbeat. Using a rubber spatula, scrape down the batter in the bowl, making sure the ingredients are well blended.

Divide the batter among the prepared pans and bake for 25–30 minutes, or until a cake tester inserted in the center of the cake comes out clean. Let the layers cool in the pans for 1 hour. Remove from the pans and cool completely on a wire rack.

To make the cream filling: In a large bowl, whip the heavy cream with the sugar and vanilla until stiff peaks form.

To make the berry filling: Gently toss the berries with the sugar to evenly coat the fruit.

To assemble the cake: When the cake layers have cooled completely, spread one-third of the whipped cream filling over the bottom cake layer, followed by one-third of the berry filling. Repeat with the remaining layers.

MAKES ONE 3-LAYER 9-INCH CAKE

Red Velvet Cake
with Creamy Vanilla Frosting

*T*his is one of our most popular cakes at the bakery. Half of the customers love it because they haven't eaten it since their grandmother made it when they were kids, and the other half because they think the red color is really neat. But everyone thinks it's delicious.

CAKE

3⅓ cups cake flour (not self-rising)
¾ cup (1½ sticks) unsalted butter, softened
2¼ cups sugar
3 large eggs, at room temperature
6 tablespoons red food coloring
3 tablespoons unsweetened cocoa
1½ teaspoons vanilla extract

1½ teaspoons salt
1½ cups buttermilk
1½ teaspoons cider vinegar
1½ teaspoons baking soda

FROSTING

1 recipe Creamy Vanilla Frosting (page 126)

Preheat oven to 350 degrees.

Grease and lightly flour three 9 x 2-inch round cake pans, then line the bottoms with waxed paper.

To make the cake: In a small bowl, sift the cake flour and set aside. In a large bowl, on the medium speed of an electric mixer, cream the butter and sugar until very light and fluffy, about 5 minutes. Add the eggs, one at a time, beating well after each addition.

In a small bowl, whisk together the red food coloring, cocoa, and vanilla. Add to the batter and beat well.

In a measuring cup, stir the salt into the buttermilk. Add to the batter in three parts, alternating with the flour. With each addition, beat until the ingredients are incorporated, but do not overbeat.

In a small bowl, stir together the cider vinegar and baking soda. Add to the batter and mix well. Using a rubber spatula, scrape down the batter in the bowl, making sure the ingredients are well blended and the batter is smooth.

Divide the batter among the prepared pans. Bake for 30–40 minutes, or until a cake tester inserted in the center of the cake comes out clean. Let the layers cool in the pans for 1 hour. Remove from the pans and cool completely on a wire rack.

When the cake has cooled, spread the frosting between the layers, then the ice top and sides of the cake with Creamy Vanilla Frosting.

MAKES ONE 3-LAYER 9-INCH CAKE

Magnolia's Vanilla Cupcakes

*E*veryone is always asking us which is the most popular cupcake at the bakery. Most people are surprised that it is what we call the vanilla vanilla—the vanilla cupcake with the vanilla icing (and the most popular color for the icing is pink).

Cupcakes
1 ½ cups self-rising flour
1 ¼ cups all-purpose flour
1 cup (2 sticks) unsalted butter,
    softened
2 cups sugar
4 large eggs, at room temperature

1 cup milk
1 teaspoon vanilla extract

Icing
Vanilla Buttercream (page 117) or
    Chocolate Buttercream (page 122)

Preheat oven to 350 degrees.

Line two 12-cup muffin tins with cupcake papers.

In a small bowl, combine the flours. Set aside.

In a large bowl, on the medium speed of an electric mixer, cream the butter until smooth. Add the sugar gradually and beat until fluffy, about 3 minutes. Add the eggs, one at a time, beating well after each addition. Add the dry ingredients in three parts, alternating with the milk and vanilla. With each addition, beat until the ingredients are incorporated but do not overbeat. Using a rubber spatula, scrape down the batter in the bowl to make sure the ingredients are well blended. Carefully spoon the batter into the cupcake liners, filling them about three-quarters full. Bake for 20–25 minutes, or until a cake tester inserted into the center of the cupcake comes out clean.

Cool the cupcakes in the tins for 15 minutes. Remove from the tins and cool completely on a wire rack before icing. At the bakery we ice the cupcakes with either Vanilla Buttercream or Chocolate Buttercream.

MAKES ABOUT 2 DOZEN CUPCAKES
(DEPENDING ON THE SIZE OF YOUR CUPCAKE PAPERS AND MUFFIN TINS)

note: If you would like to make a layer cake intead of cupcakes, divide the batter between two 9-inch round cake pans and bake the layers for 30–40 minutes.

Devil's Food Cake with Seven-Minute Icing and Coconut

*T*his is the same recipe we've made in my family for every birthday since the beginning of time, and the same cake we serve at the bakery—but a different icing and the coconut garnish give it a whole new taste.

Cake
3 cups all-purpose flour
1 ½ teaspoons baking powder
1 ½ teaspoons baking soda
¾ teaspoon salt
¾ cup (1 ½ sticks) unsalted butter, softened
2 cups firmly packed light brown sugar
3 large eggs, separated, at room temperature (see first Note)

9 ounces unsweetened chocolate, melted (see second Note)
2 cups milk
1 ½ teaspoons vanilla extract

Icing
One recipe Seven-Minute Icing (page 125)

Garnish
Sweetened shredded coconut

Notes:

It is best to separate the eggs when cold and then allow them to come to room temperature before proceeding with the recipe.

To melt the chocolate, place in a double boiler over simmering water on low heat for approximately 5–10 minutes. Stir occasionally until completely smooth and no pieces of chocolate remain. Remove from the heat and let cool to lukewarm, 5–10 minutes.

Preheat oven to 350 degrees.

Grease and lightly flour three 9 x 2-inch round cake pans, then line the bottoms with waxed paper.

In a small bowl, sift together the flour, baking powder, baking soda, and salt. Set aside.

In a large bowl, on the medium speed of an electric mixer, cream the butter until smooth. Add the sugar and beat until fluffy, about 3 minutes.

In a separate small bowl, beat the egg yolks until thick and lemon-colored, about 2 minutes. Add the beaten yolks to the butter mixture and beat well. Add the chocolate, mixing until well incorporated. Add the dry ingredients in three parts, alternating with the milk and vanilla. With each addition, beat until the ingredients are incorporated, but do not overbeat. Using a rubber spatula, scrape down the batter in the bowl, making sure the ingredients are well blended and the batter is smooth.

In a separate small bowl, beat the egg whites on the high speed of an electric mixer until soft peaks form. Gently fold into the batter. Divide the batter among the prepared pans and bake for 30–35 minutes, or until a cake tester inserted in the center of the cake comes out clean.

Let the layers cool in the pans for 1 hour. Remove from the pans and cool completely on a wire rack.

When the cake has cooled, ice between the layers, then ice the top and sides of the cake with Seven-Minute Icing. Sprinkle the top of the cake generously with the coconut.

MAKES ONE 3-LAYER 9-INCH CAKE

Banana Cake with White Chocolate Cream Cheese Icing

*T*his recipe came about because I wanted to make a banana cake using butter instead of the traditional oil as the shortening. The result is a cake with a very different and quite lovely texture, and it's perfectly complemented by the white chocolate icing.

CAKE

3 cups cake flour (not self-rising)
1 teaspoon baking soda
³/₄ teaspoon salt
¹/₂ teaspoon baking powder
1 cup (2 sticks) unsalted butter, softened
2 cups sugar
3 large eggs, at room temperature
1¹/₂ cups mashed very ripe bananas

6 tablespoons buttermilk
1¹/₂ teaspoons vanilla extract

ICING

1 recipe White Chocolate Cream Cheese Icing (page 127)

GARNISH

³/₄ cup chopped walnuts or walnut halves

Preheat oven to 325 degrees.

Grease and lightly flour two 9 x 2-inch round cake pans, then line the bottoms with waxed paper.

To make the cake: In a small bowl, sift together the flour, baking soda, salt, and baking powder. Set aside.

In a large bowl, on the medium speed of an electric mixer, cream the butter until smooth. Add the sugar gradually and beat until fluffy, about 3 minutes. Add the eggs, one at a time, beating well after each addition. Add the bananas. Add half of the dry ingredients, mixing until well incorporated, then add the buttermilk and vanilla, and then the second half of the dry ingredients, mixing well. Divide the batter between the prepared pans. Bake for 40–50 minutes, or until a cake tester inserted in the center of the cake comes out clean.

Let the layers cool in the pans for 1 hour. Remove from the pans and cool completely on a wire rack.

When the cake has cooled, ice between the layers with White Chocolate Cream Cheese Icing, then ice the top and sides of the cake. Garnish with the walnuts as desired.

MAKES ONE 2-LAYER 9-INCH CAKE

Caramel Pecan Layer Cake

A light, moist vanilla cake iced with creamy caramel frosting and generous amounts of toasted pecans. It is a wonderful birthday cake alternative if you want to serve something different from the traditional yellow or chocolate cake.

CAKE
1 ½ cups self-rising flour
1 ¼ cups all-purpose flour
1 cup (2 sticks) unsalted butter, softened
2 cups sugar
4 large eggs, at room temperature
1 cup milk

1 teaspoon vanilla extract

ICING
1 recipe Caramel Frosting (page 119)

GARNISH
1 ½ cups coarsely chopped toasted pecans (see Note)

Note: To toast the pecans, place on a baking sheet in a 350-degree oven for 15 minutes, or until lightly browned and fragrant.

Preheat oven to 350 degrees.

Grease and lightly flour three 9 x 2-inch round cake pans, then line the bottoms with waxed paper.

To make the cake: In a small bowl, combine the flours and set aside. In a large bowl, on the medium speed of an electric mixer, cream the butter until smooth. Add the sugar gradually and beat until fluffy, about 3 minutes. Add the eggs, one at a time, beating well after each addition. Add the dry ingredients in three parts, alternating with the milk and vanilla. With each addition, beat until the ingredients are incorporated, but do not overbeat. Using a rubber spatula, scrape down the batter in the bowl, making sure the ingredients are well blended.

Divide the batter among the prepared pans and bake for 25–30 minutes, or until a cake tester inserted in the center of the cake comes out clean. Let the layers cool in the pans for 1 hour. Remove from the pans and cool completely on a wire rack.

When the layers have cooled completely, ice the cake by filling between the layers first with Caramel Frosting and then sprinkling with one-third of the pecans on each layer. Then ice the top and sides, and sprinkle the top with the remaining pecans.

MAKES ONE 3-LAYER 9-INCH CAKE

Magnolia's Chocolate Cupcakes

Made from the same batter as our popular Chocolate Buttermilk Cake, this not too rich and not too chocolatey cupcake goes equally well with the vanilla or chocolate buttercream icing.

CUPCAKES
2 cups all-purpose flour
1 teaspoon baking soda
1 cup (2 sticks) unsalted butter, softened
1 cup granulated sugar
1 cup firmly packed light brown sugar
4 large eggs, at room temperature

6 ounces unsweetened chocolate, melted (see Note)
1 cup buttermilk
1 teaspoon vanilla extract

ICINGS
Vanilla Buttercream (page 117) or Chocolate Buttercream (page 122)

Note: To melt the chocolate, place in a double boiler over simmering water on low heat for approximately 5–10 minutes. Stir occasionally until completely smooth and no pieces of chocolate remain. Remove from the heat and let cool to lukewarm 5–10 minutes.

Preheat oven to 350 degrees.

Line two 12-cup muffin tins with cupcake papers. Set aside.

In a small bowl, sift together the flour and baking soda. Set aside.

In a large bowl, on the medium speed of an electric mixer, cream the butter until smooth. Add the sugars and beat until fluffy, about 3 minutes. Add the eggs, one at a time, beating well after each addition. Add the chocolate, mixing until well incorporated. Add the dry ingredients in three parts, alternating with the buttermilk and vanilla. With each addition, beat until the ingredients are incorporated, but do not overbeat. Using a rubber spatula, scrape down the batter in the bowl to make sure the ingredients are well blended and the batter is smooth. Carefully spoon the batter into the cupcake liners, filling them about three-quarters full. Bake for 20–25 minutes, or until a cake tester inserted in the center of the cupcake comes out clean.

Cool the cupcakes in the tins for 15 minutes. Remove from the tins and cool completely on a wire rack before icing. At the bakery we ice the cupcakes with either Vanilla Buttercream or Chocolate Buttercream.

MAKES ABOUT 2 DOZEN CUPCAKES
(DEPENDING ON THE SIZE OF YOUR CUPCAKE PAPERS AND MUFFIN TINS)

note: If you would like to make a layer cake intead of cupcakes, divide the batter between two 9-inch round cake pans and bake the layers for 30–40 minutes.

Carrot Cake

We don't make carrot cake at the bakery (I can just hear the Hummingbird cake fans screaming), but this is the cake I make most often at home. We love it.

CAKE
2 cups all-purpose flour
1 teaspoon baking powder
1 teaspoon cinnamon
$^1/_2$ teaspoon salt
1 cup vegetable oil (preferably canola)
1 $^3/_4$ cups sugar
3 large eggs, at room temperature
1 $^1/_2$ teaspoons vanilla extract
2 cups lightly packed shredded carrots
One 8-ounce can crushed pineapple in its own juice, with juice

1 cup coarsely chopped toasted pecans (see Note)
$^3/_4$ cup sweetened shredded coconut

ICING
1 recipe Cream Cheese Icing (page 118)

GARNISH
Coarsely chopped toasted pecans (see Note)

$Note:$ To toast the pecans, place on a baking sheet in a 350-degree oven for 15 minutes, or until lightly browned and fragrant.

Preheat oven to 325 degrees.

Grease and lightly flour two 9 x 2-inch round cake pans, then line the bottoms with waxed paper.

In a small bowl, sift together the flour, baking powder, cinnamon, and salt. Set aside.

In a large bowl, on the medium speed of an electric mixer, beat together the oil and sugar. Add the eggs, one at a time, and beat until light and thick, about 2 minutes. Add the vanilla and beat well. Gradually add the dry ingredients, beating until well incorporated. Stir in the carrots, pineapple and juice, pecans, and coconut. Divide the batter between the prepared pans and bake for 40–50 minutes, or until a cake tester inserted in the center of the cake comes out clean. Let the layers cool in the pans for 1 hour. Remove from the pans and cool completely on a wire rack.

When the cake has cooled, ice between the layers, then ice the top and sides of the cake with Cream Cheese Icing. Garnish with the toasted pecans as desired.

MAKES ONE 2-LAYER 9-INCH CAKE

Devil's Food Cupcakes
with Caramel Frosting

I love devil's food, so I thought a second recipe seemed like a really good idea. This recipe is very different from the devil's food cake recipe—more chocolatey and extremely light in texture. These cupcakes are great with the caramel frosting, but I wouldn't hesitate to try them with other icings as well.

CUPCAKES

2 cups cake flour (not self-rising)
1 cup unsweetened Dutch process cocoa
1 1/2 teaspoons baking soda
1/2 teaspoon salt
3/4 cup (1 1/2 sticks) unsalted butter, softened

1 1/2 cups firmly packed light brown sugar
1/2 cup granulated sugar
3 large eggs, at room temperature
1 1/2 cups buttermilk
2 teaspoons vanilla extract

FROSTING

1 recipe Caramel Frosting (page 119)

Preheat oven to 350 degrees.

Line three 12-cup muffin tins with cupcake papers. Set aside.

In a small bowl, sift together the flour, cocoa, baking soda, and salt. Set aside.

In a large bowl, on the medium speed of an electric mixer, cream the butter until smooth. Add the sugars and beat until fluffy, about 3 minutes. Add the eggs, one at a time, beating well after each addition. Add the dry ingredients in three parts, alternating with the buttermilk and vanilla. With each addition, beat until the ingredients are incorporated, but do not overbeat. Using a rubber spatula, scrape down the batter in the bowl, making sure the ingredients are well blended. Carefully spoon the batter into the cupcake liners, filling them about three-quarters full. Bake for 25–30 minutes, or until a cake tester inserted in the center of the cupcake comes out clean.

Cool the cupcakes in the tins for 15 minutes. Remove from the tins and cool completely on a wire rack before icing with Caramel Frosting.

MAKES ABOUT 2 1/2 DOZEN CUPCAKES
(DEPENDING ON THE SIZE OF YOUR CUPCAKE PAPERS AND MUFFIN TINS)

Apple Cake with Butterscotch Cream Cheese Frosting

A fluffy, golden cake with chunks of apples and a sweet, creamy frosting. If you're not a butterscotch fan, this cake is also good iced with vanilla buttercream.

CAKE

3 cups all-purpose flour
2 teaspoons baking powder
$1/2$ teaspoon salt
1 cup (2 sticks) unsalted butter, softened
2 cups sugar
5 large eggs, at room temperature
1 cup milk

$1 1/2$ teaspoons vanilla extract
$3 1/2$ cups coarsely chopped, peeled, crisp tart apples (such as Winesap or Macoun)

FROSTING

1 recipe Butterscotch Cream Cheese Frosting (page 123)

Preheat oven to 325 degrees.

Grease and lightly flour two 9-inch round cake pans, then line the bottoms with waxed paper.

In a small bowl, sift together the flour, baking powder, and salt. Set aside. In a large bowl, on the medium speed of an electric mixer, cream the butter until smooth. Add the sugar gradually and beat until fluffy, about 3 minutes. Add the eggs, one at a time, beating well after each addition. Add the dry ingredients in three parts, alternating with the milk and vanilla. With each addition, beat until the ingredients are incorporated, but do not overbeat. Using a rubber spatula, scrape down the batter in the bowl, making sure the ingredients are well blended. Stir in the apples.

Divide the batter between the prepared pans. Bake for 40–50 minutes, or until a cake tester inserted in the center of the cake comes out clean.

Let the layers cool in the pans for 1 hour. Remove from the pans and cool completely on a wire rack.

When the cake has cooled, ice between the layers, then ice top and sides of cake with Butterscotch Cream Cheese Frosting.

MAKES ONE 2-LAYER 9-INCH CAKE

Ice Creams and
Icebox Desserts

White Chocolate Peanut Brittle Ice Cream

*T*his has been our most popular ice cream flavor both at the bakery and in grocery stores since we launched our ice cream line in 2001. The peanut brittle complements the brown-sugar-based custard perfectly.

3 large egg yolks, at room temperature

2 cups half-and-half

2/3 cup firmly packed light brown sugar

3 tablespoons light corn syrup

1 tablespoon vanilla extract

1 1/4 cups coarsely chopped peanut bars (preferably Planters)

1/2 cup coarsely chopped white chocolate (preferably Lindt)

In a medium-size bowl, with an eggbeater or a whisk, beat the egg yolks until creamy, 2–3 minutes. Set aside.

In a medium saucepan, combine the half-and-half, sugar, and syrup, and cook over medium heat, stirring constantly, until the sugar is completely dissolved. Remove from the heat and add 1/2 cup of the cream mixture to the egg yolks, stirring to warm the egg yolks. Return the entire mixture to the pot and continue to cook, stirring constantly, until it coats the back of the spoon, about 10 minutes. Remove from the heat and place the pot in a bowl of cold water. When the custard has cooled to room temperature, stir in the vanilla. Cover and refrigerate until completely chilled, preferably overnight.

Pour into an ice cream machine and freeze until partially set, about 20 minutes. Stir in the chopped peanut bars and white chocolate, and continue freezing until firm, following the manufacturer's instructions.

MAKES 1 QUART

Old-fashioned Chocolate Chip Ice Cream

I've been making this ice cream since I was a child and we got our first ice cream machine. It's always been both my dad and my brother's favorite flavor.

6 large egg yolks, at room
    temperature
²/₃ cup sugar
2 cups half-and-half

1 cup heavy cream
1 tablespoon vanilla extract
1 cup miniature semisweet chocolate
    chips

In a medium-size bowl, with an eggbeater or a whisk, beat the egg yolks until creamy, 2–3 minutes. Add the sugar and beat until incorporated. Set aside.

In a double boiler over simmering water, heat the half-and-half until scalded. Add ½ cup of the half-and-half to the egg mixture, stirring to warm the egg yolks. Return the entire mixture to the double boiler and continue to cook, stirring constantly, until the mixture coats the back of a spoon, about 10 minutes. Remove from the heat and place the pot in a bowl of cold water. When the custard has cooled to room temperature, stir in the heavy cream and vanilla. Cover and refrigerate until completely chilled, preferably overnight.

Pour into an ice cream machine and freeze until partially set, about 20 minutes. Stir in the chocolate chips and continue freezing until firm, following the manufacturer's instructions.

MAKES 1 QUART

Vanilla Sandwich Creme Cookie Ice Cream

For vanilla lovers like myself, this is like the well-known "cookies and cream" or "Oreo" ice creams, but it is made with vanilla cookies instead of chocolate. It's another big favorite at the bakery.

6 large egg yolks, at room temperature
²⁄₃ cup sugar
2 cups half-and-half
1 cup heavy cream

1 tablespoon vanilla extract
12 vanilla sandwich cookies (such as Nabisco or Famous Amos), broken into quarters

In a medium-size bowl, with an eggbeater or a whisk, beat the egg yolks until creamy, 2–3 minutes. Add the sugar and beat until incorporated. Set aside.

In a double boiler over simmering water, heat the half-and-half until scalded. Add ½ cup of the half-and-half to the egg mixture, stirring to warm the egg yolks. Return the entire mixture to the double boiler and continue to cook, stirring constantly, until the mixture coats the back of a spoon, about 10 minutes. Remove from the heat and place the pot in a bowl of cold water. When the custard has cooled to room temperature, stir in the cream and vanilla. Cover and refrigerate until completely chilled, preferably overnight.

Pour into an ice cream machine and freeze until partially set, about 20 minutes. Stir in the broken cookie pieces and continue freezing until firm, following the manufacturer's instructions.

MAKES 1 QUART

Caramel Toffee Pecan Icebox Pie

A brown sugar shortbread crust, a creamy caramel filling, and a topping of Heath bars and toasted pecans—I don't think one could want much more in an icebox dessert.

CRUST
2/3 cup all-purpose flour
1/3 cup firmly packed light brown sugar
2/3 cup chopped toasted pecans (see Note)
6 tablespoons (3/4 stick) unsalted butter, softened and cut into small pieces

FILLING
12 ounces vanilla caramels

3 tablespoons heavy cream
3/4 pound (one and a half 8-ounce packages) cream cheese, softened
3/4 cup heavy cream, whipped to stiff peaks

GARNISH
1/3 cup chopped Heath bars (or any chocolate-covered toffee bars)
1/3 cup chopped toasted pecans (see Note)

Note: To toast the pecans, place on a baking sheet in a 350-degree oven for 15 minutes, or until lightly browned and fragrant.

Preheat oven to 325 degrees.

To make the crust: In a medium-size bowl, combine the flour, sugar, and pecans. Using a pastry blender, cut in the butter until the mixture resembles coarse crumbs. Press into the bottom of a 9-inch pie dish. Bake for 12–15 minutes, or until lightly golden. Remove from the oven and allow to cool to room temperature, about 45 minutes.

To make the filling: In a medium-size saucepan over low heat, melt the caramels with the 3 tablespoons of cream, stirring occasionally until smooth. Remove from the heat and allow to cool to room temperature, about 30 minutes.

In a large bowl, on the medium speed of an electric mixer, beat the cream cheese until smooth. Add the cooled caramel and beat well.

In a separate bowl, beat the ¾ cup of heavy cream until stiff peaks form. Gently fold the whipped cream into the cream cheese mixture until well blended and no streaks of cream remain. Spoon the filling into the cooled crust.

To garnish, sprinkle the Heath bars and pecans around the edge of the pie. Cover with plastic wrap and chill overnight in the refrigerator before serving.

MAKES ONE 9-INCH PIE

Heavenly Hash
Ice Cream Pie

*H*eavenly Hash was one of my favorite flavors of ice cream when I was growing up. It's really difficult to find these days, so I decided to put the ingredients together in an ice cream pie and give up my supermarket search. You can use chocolate or vanilla ice cream in this recipe (or a layer of each)—both versions are great.

CRUST
1/2 cup (1 stick) unsalted butter,
   melted
2 cups chocolate wafer crumbs

MARSHMALLOW SAUCE
4 cups miniature marshmallows
1/3 cup heavy cream

FILLING
1 quart chocolate ice cream
3/4 cup coarsely chopped toasted
   almonds (see Note)
1/4 cup miniature semisweet chocolate
   chips

Note: To toast the almonds, place on a baking sheet in a 350-degree oven for 15 minutes, or until lightly browned and fragrant.

To make the crust: In a medium-size bowl, combine the butter and wafer crumbs. Press firmly into a lightly buttered 9-inch pie dish. Cover tightly with plastic wrap and place in the freezer for 1 hour.

To make the marshmallow sauce: In the top of a double boiler over barely simmering water, combine the marshmallows with the cream. Stir until the marshmallows are completely melted and the sauce is smooth, 3–5 minutes. Remove from the heat and transfer the sauce to a glass measuring cup. Allow to cool for 20 minutes.

Meanwhile, transfer the ice cream from the freezer to a covered plastic storage container and place in the refrigerator to soften for 20 minutes.

Remove the piecrust from the freezer and the ice cream from the refrigerator. Using a wooden spoon, stir the ice cream until creamy and of good spreading consistency. Spread half of the ice cream over the bottom of the prepared crust. (I recommend using a small offset icing spatula if you have one.) Pour the marshmallow sauce evenly over the ice cream and sprinkle with half of the almonds. Cover tightly with plastic wrap and place in the freezer for 15 minutes to set. (Place the remaining ice cream in the freezer as well so that it doesn't get too soft.)

Remove the pie and ice cream from the freezer and carefully spread the remaining ice cream evenly over the first layer. To garnish, sprinkle the remaining almonds and the chocolate chips around the edge of the pie. Cover tightly with plastic wrap and then aluminum foil, and freeze until the pie is firm, at least 4 hours or overnight.

Let the pie soften slightly at room temperature, about 10 minutes, before slicing and serving.

MAKES ONE 9-INCH PIE

Cherry Jamboree

We started making this at the bakery a few years ago when a staff member remarked that her grandmother made a dessert just like our cream cheese chocolate pudding squares but with cherry pie filling instead. It turned out to be even more popular with our customers, and so we're still making it.

CRUST
1 cup all-purpose flour
½ cup chopped toasted pecans (see Note)
⅓ cup (5⅓ tablespoons) unsalted butter, melted

CREAM CHEESE FILLING
½ pound (1 eight-ounce package) cream cheese, softened

1 cup confectioners' sugar, sifted
1 cup heavy cream

TOPPING
One 21-ounce can cherry pie filling

GARNISH
Sweet Vanilla Whipped Cream (page 121)
Toasted pecan halves (see Note)

Note: To toast the pecans, place on a baking sheet in a 350-degree oven for 15 minutes, or until lightly browned and fragrant.

Preheat oven to 375 degrees.

To make the crust: In a small bowl, combine the flour, pecans, and butter. Press firmly into the bottom of an ungreased 8 x 8-inch glass baking dish. Bake for 15 minutes. Remove from the oven and allow to cool on a wire rack.

To make the filling: In a large bowl, on the low speed of an electric mixer, beat the cream cheese until smooth, about 2 minutes. Add the sugar and beat well. In a separate small bowl, beat the heavy cream until stiff peaks form. Gently fold the whipped cream into the cream cheese mixture.

When the crust has cooled, spread the cream cheese filling evenly over the crust using a rubber spatula. Spread the cherry pie filling on top. Cover with plastic wrap and chill for at least 2 hours or overnight. Cut into squares and serve with a dollop of whipped cream and the pecan halves.

MAKES NINE 2½-INCH SQUARES

Magnolia's Famous Banana Pudding

I started making this pudding when I was in my early twenties and cooking at a Tex-Mex restaurant and bar. Customers loved it, so when we opened the bakery many years later, it seemed like a great idea to serve it there. It remains the second most popular dessert (after the cupcakes) at the bakery.

One 14-ounce can sweetened condensed milk

1 ½ cups ice cold water

One 3.4-ounce package instant vanilla pudding mix (preferably Jell-O brand)

3 cups heavy cream

One 12-ounce box Nabisco Nilla Wafers (no substitutions!)

4 cups sliced ripe bananas

In a small bowl, on the medium speed of an electric mixer, beat together the sweetened condensed milk and water until well combined, about 1 minute. Add the pudding mix and beat well, about 2 minutes more. Cover and refrigerate for 3–4 hours or overnight, before continuing. It is very important to allow the proper amount of time for the pudding mixture to set.

In a large bowl, on the medium speed of an electric mixer, whip the heavy cream until stiff peaks form. Gently fold the pudding mixture into the whipped cream until well blended and no streaks of pudding remain.

To assemble the dessert, select a large, wide bowl (preferably glass) with a 4–5-quart capacity. Arrange one-third of the wafers to cover the bottom of the bowl, overlapping if necessary, then one-third of the bananas and one-third of the pudding. Repeat the layering twice more, garnishing with additional wafers or wafer crumbs on the top layer of the pudding. Cover tightly with plastic wrap and allow to chill in the refrigerator for 4 hours—or up to 8 hours, but no longer!—before serving.

SERVES 12–15

Lemon Pudding with Raspberries and Gingersnaps

*M*agnolia day manager Margaret Hathaway came up with this delightful spring-time dessert that is based on our banana pudding.

8 large egg yolks, at room
  temperature
2 cups sugar
$\frac{1}{2}$ cup cornstarch
3 cups warm water
$\frac{1}{2}$ cup (1 stick) unsalted butter,
  melted and cooled to room
  temperature

$1\frac{1}{2}$ cups fresh lemon juice
1 teaspoon grated lemon zest
3 cups heavy cream
12 ounces gingersnap cookies (any
  popular boxed brand is fine)
1 pint fresh raspberries

In a medium-size bowl, with an eggbeater or a whisk, beat the egg yolks until creamy, 2–3 minutes. Set aside.

In a large saucepan, combine the sugar and cornstarch. Gradually add the water and cook over medium heat, stirring constantly, until the mixture thickens, about 5 minutes.

Remove from the heat and add 2 cups of the hot mixture to the egg yolks, stirring to warm the egg yolks. Return the entire mixture to the pot and heat 1 minute more.

Remove from the heat and stir in the butter, lemon juice, and lemon zest. Transfer to a medium-size bowl and cool to room temperature, about 1 hour.

In a large bowl, on the medium speed of an electric mixer, whip the cream until stiff peaks form. Gently fold the pudding mixture into the whipped cream until well blended and no streaks of pudding remain.

To assemble the dessert, select a large, wide bowl (preferably glass) with a 4–5-quart capacity. Arrange one-third of the gingersnaps to cover the bottom of the bowl, overlapping if necessary, then one-third of the pudding. Repeat the layering twice more. Garnish the top layer with raspberries. Cover tightly with plastic wrap and allow to chill in the refrigerator for 4 hours—or up to 8 hours, but no longer!—before serving.

SERVES 12–15

Icings, Frostings, and Sauces

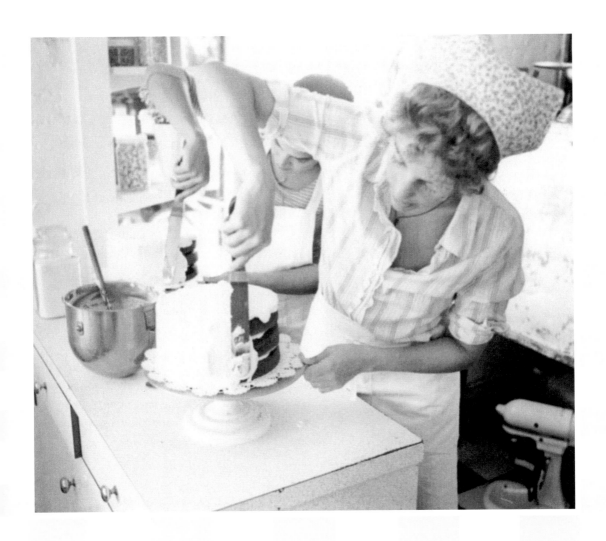

Vanilla Buttercream

The vanilla buttercream we use at the bakery is technically not a buttercream but actually an old-fashioned confectioners' sugar and butter frosting. Be sure to beat the icing for the amount of time called for in the recipe to achieve the desired creamy texture.

1 cup (2 sticks) unsalted butter,
    softened
6–8 cups confectioners' sugar

½ cup milk
2 teaspoons vanilla extract

Place the butter in a large mixing bowl. Add 4 cups of the sugar and then the milk and vanilla. On the medium speed of an electric mixer, beat until smooth and creamy, about 3–5 minutes. Gradually add the remaining sugar, 1 cup at a time, beating well after each addition (about 2 minutes), until the icing is thick enough to be of good spreading consistency. You may not need to add all of the sugar. If desired, add a few drops of food coloring and mix thoroughly. (Use and store the icing at room temperature because icing will set if chilled.) Icing can be stored in an airtight container for up to 3 days.

MAKES ENOUGH FOR ONE 2-LAYER 9-INCH CAKE OR 2 DOZEN CUPCAKES

note: If you are icing a 3-layer cake, use the following recipe proportions:

1½ cups (3 sticks) unsalted butter
8–10 cups confectioners' sugar

¾ cup milk
1 tablespoon vanilla extract

Cream Cheese Icing

*C*ream cheese icing is probably my favorite icing, and I haven't yet found anyone who doesn't like it. It's the traditional icing for carrot cake, but is delicious with many other desserts as well.

1 pound (two 8-ounce packages) cream cheese, softened and cut into small pieces

6 tablespoons unsalted butter, softened and cut into small pieces
1 ½ teaspoons vanilla extract
5 cups sifted confectioners' sugar

In a large bowl, on the medium speed of an electric mixer, beat the cream cheese and butter until smooth, about 3 minutes. Add the vanilla and beat well. Gradually add the sugar, 1 cup at a time, beating continuously until smooth and creamy. Cover and refrigerate icing for 2 to 3 hours, but no longer, to thicken before using.

MAKES ENOUGH FOR ONE 2- OR 3-LAYER 9-INCH CAKE

Caramel Frosting

I love anything with caramel, and I always wanted to make an easy caramel frosting that didn't involve a candy thermometer. Here it is. (This icing tastes better if made the day before the cake because the brown sugar gives the icing a slightly grainy texture that improves if allowed to set overnight.)

2 cups (4 sticks) unsalted butter,
   softened
5 cups sifted confectioners' sugar
1½ cups firmly packed light brown
   sugar

½ cup milk
2 tablespoons dark corn syrup
2 teaspoons vanilla extract

In a large bowl, on the medium speed of an electric mixer, cream the butter until smooth. Add the sugars and beat on low speed for 2 minutes. Add the milk, syrup, and vanilla, and beat until smooth and creamy, 3–5 minutes. Use immediately or store, covered, at room temperature for up to 2 days.

MAKES ENOUGH FOR ONE 3-LAYER 9-INCH CAKE OR 3 DOZEN CUPCAKES

White Chocolate Buttercream

I'm one of those people who prefers white chocolate to chocolate, and the visual contrast of the white icing with a chocolate or devil's food cake is wonderful.

1 ½ cups (3 sticks) unsalted butter, softened
6 tablespoons milk
9 ounces white chocolate, melted and cooled to lukewarm (see Note)

1 teaspoon vanilla extract
3 cups sifted confectioners' sugar

Note: To melt the chocolate, place in a double boiler over simmering water on low heat for about 5–10 minutes. Stir occasionally until completely smooth and no pieces of chocolate remain. Remove from the heat and let cool for 5–15 minutes, or until lukewarm.

In a large bowl, on the medium speed of an electric mixer, beat the butter until creamy, about 3 minutes. Add the milk carefully and beat until smooth. Add the melted chocolate and beat well, about 2 minutes. Add the vanilla and beat for 3 minutes. Gradually add the sugar and beat on low speed until creamy and of desired consistency.

MAKES ENOUGH FOR ONE 2-LAYER 9-INCH CAKE OR 2 DOZEN CUPCAKES

Note: If you are icing a 3-layer cake, use the following recipe proportions:

2 cups (4 sticks) unsalted butter
½ cup milk
12 ounces white chocolate

1 ½ teaspoons vanilla extract
4 cups sifted confectioners' sugar

Sweet Vanilla Whipped Cream

I believe that no pie is complete without a large dollop of whipped cream to accompany it. Since I suggest it so often in my recipes, I thought I should include my version of not-too-sweet whipped cream.

2 cups heavy cream

2 teaspoons sugar

2 teaspoons vanilla extract

Place all the ingredients in a medium-size bowl and whip with an eggbeater or a whisk until soft peaks form. Serve immediately with your favorite dessert, or cover tightly with plastic wrap and refrigerate for up to 4 hours.

Chocolate Buttercream

The key to achieving the same creamy texture that we do at the bakery is in beating the icing at the proper speeds for the proper amount of time. If beaten at too high a speed, the icing incorporates a lot of air and becomes fluffy rather than creamy.

1 ½ cups (3 sticks) unsalted butter, softened
2 tablespoons milk
9 ounces semisweet chocolate, melted and cooled to lukewarm (see Note)

1 teaspoon vanilla extract
2 ¼ cups sifted confectioners' sugar

Note: To melt the chocolate, place in a double boiler over simmering water on low heat for about 5–10 minutes. Stir occasionally until completely smooth and no pieces of chocolate remain. Remove from the heat and let cool for 5–15 minutes, or until lukewarm.

In a large bowl, on the medium speed of an electric mixer, beat the butter until creamy, about 3 minutes. Add the milk carefully and beat until smooth. Add the melted chocolate and beat well, about 2 minutes. Add the vanilla and beat for 3 minutes. Gradually add the sugar and beat on low speed until creamy and of desired consistency.

MAKES ENOUGH FOR ONE 2-LAYER 9-INCH CAKE OR 2 DOZEN CUPCAKES

Note: If you are icing a 3-layer cake, use the following recipe proportions:

2 cups (4 sticks) unsalted butter
3 tablespoons milk
12 ounces semisweet chocolate

1 ½ teaspoons vanilla extract
3 cups confectioners' sugar

Butterscotch Cream Cheese Frosting

This not-so-sweet frosting combines a deep butterscotch flavor with the tanginess of the cream cheese. It goes just wonderfully with the apple layer cake.

1 pound (two 8-ounce packages) cream cheese, softened
6 tablespoons unsalted butter, softened

1 cup firmly packed light brown sugar
2 tablespoons dark corn syrup
1 teaspoon vanilla extract

In a large bowl, on the medium speed of an electric mixer, beat the cream cheese and butter until smooth, about 3 minutes. Add the sugar, corn syrup, and vanilla, and beat until smooth and creamy.

Cover and refrigerate frosting for 1 hour to thicken before using.

MAKES ENOUGH FOR ONE 2- OR 3-LAYER 9-INCH CAKE

Caramel Sauce

*C*aramel is not difficult to prepare, but it has to be done correctly. Pay attention as it nears the end of cooking because it can go from deep amber to burnt very, very quickly.

1 cup cold water
3 cups sugar

2 cups heavy cream, at room
temperature

In a medium-size saucepan, combine the water and sugar. Set over medium-low heat, stirring occasionally, until the sugar dissolves, about 3 minutes, making sure no sugar is sticking to the sides of the pan. Increase the heat to high and boil without stirring until the syrup becomes a deep amber color, about 15 minutes. To prevent the syrup from becoming grainy, use a pastry brush dipped into cold water to brush down any sugar crystals sticking to the sides of the pan. Swirl the pan occasionally for even browning.

Once the syrup turns deep amber in color, immediately remove from the heat. Slowly and carefully add the cream to the syrup (the mixture will bubble vigorously), whisking constantly until the cream is incorporated.

Return the pan to medium-low heat and stir until the sauce is smooth, about 1 minute.

Remove from the heat and allow to come to room temperature before refrigerating. The caramel can be stored for up to 1 month in the refrigerator.

MAKES 3 ½ CUPS

Seven-Minute Icing

This classic American marshmallow-like frosting is a childhood favorite of many. It is a cooked icing but is relatively simple to make and can be used to frost a wide variety of cakes.

3 egg whites
2¼ cups sugar
½ cup cold water

1½ tablespoons light corn syrup
⅛ teaspoon salt
1½ teaspoons vanilla extract

Combine the egg whites, sugar, water, syrup, and salt in the top of a double boiler and place over rapidly boiling water. On the high speed of an electric mixer, beat constantly for 6–8 minutes, or until the icing stands up in soft peaks. Remove from the heat, add the vanilla, and beat about 1 minute more, or until the icing has the desired spreading consistency. Use immediately.

MAKES ENOUGH FOR ONE 2- OR 3-LAYER 9-INCH CAKE

Creamy Vanilla Frosting

*T*his silky smooth frosting is made by beating together softened butter and sugar with a thick, saucelike base. Be sure to follow the recipe directions exactly.

6 tablespoons all-purpose flour
2 cups milk
2 cups (4 sticks) unsalted butter,
   softened

2 cups sugar
2 teaspoons vanilla extract

In a medium-size saucepan, whisk the flour into the milk until smooth. Place over medium heat and, stirring constantly, cook until the mixture becomes very thick and begins to bubble, 10–15 minutes. Cover with waxed paper placed directly on the surface and cool to room temperature, about 30 minutes.

In a large bowl, on the medium high speed of an electric mixer, beat the butter for 3 minutes, until smooth and creamy. Gradually add the sugar, beating continuously for 3 minutes until fluffy. Add the vanilla and beat well.

Add the cooled milk mixture, and continue to beat on the medium high speed for 5 minutes, until very smooth and noticeably whiter in color. Cover and refrigerate for 15 minutes (no less and no longer—set a timer!). Use immediately.

MAKES ENOUGH FOR ONE 3-LAYER 9-INCH CAKE

White Chocolate Cream Cheese Icing

*W*hat can I say—white chocolate and cream cheese together in a fabulous icing that's just perfect with the banana layer cake. (It's also really good on the devil's food cupcakes.)

1 pound (two 8-ounce packages) cream cheese, softened

6 tablespoons unsalted butter, softened

1 teaspoon vanilla extract

8 ounces white chocolate (such as Lindt—do not use a baking chocolate like Callebaut), melted and cooled to lukewarm temperature (see Note)

Note: To melt the chocolate, place in a double boiler over simmering water on low heat for about 5–10 minutes. Stir occasionally until completely smooth and no pieces of chocolate remain. Remove from heat and let cool for 5–15 minutes, or until lukewarm.

In a large bowl, on the medium speed of an electric mixer, beat together the cream cheese and butter until smooth, about 3 minutes. Add the vanilla and beat well. Add the melted chocolate, and beat well. Use immediately or store, covered, at room temperature for up to 4 hours.

MAKES ENOUGH FOR ONE 2-LAYER 9-INCH CAKE

Metric Equivalencies

LIQUID AND DRY MEASURE EQUIVALENCIES

CUSTOMARY	METRIC
¼ teaspoon	1.25 milliliters
½ teaspoon	2.5 milliliters
1 teaspoon	5 milliliters
1 tablespoon	15 milliliters
1 fluid ounce	30 milliliters
¼ cup	60 milliliters
⅓ cup	80 milliliters
½ cup	120 milliliters
1 cup	240 milliliters
1 pint *(2 cups)*	480 milliliters
1 quart *(4 cups, 32 ounces)*	960 milliliters *(.96 liter)*
1 gallon *(4 quarts)*	3.84 liters
1 ounce *(by weight)*	28 grams
¼ pound *(4 ounces)*	114 grams
1 pound *(16 ounces)*	454 grams
2.2 pounds	1 kilogram *(1,000 grams)*

OVEN-TEMPERATURE EQUIVALENCIES

DESCRIPTION	°FAHRENHEIT	°CELSIUS
Cool	200	90
Very slow	250	120
Slow	300–325	150–160
Moderately slow	325–350	160–180
Moderate	350–375	180–190
Moderately hot	375–400	190–200
Hot	400–450	200–230
Very hot	450–500	230–260

Index

About the Author

Allysa Torey opened the Magnolia Bakery in New York City's Greenwich Village in the summer of 1996. Allysa, when she wasn't baking, could formerly be found around town singing with her fifties' jazz band, The Allysa Torey Swing Band. Coauthor of *The Magnolia Bakery Cookbook,* she currently lives in upstate New York with her boyfriend, Tadhg, where she spends her time writing, cooking, gardening, and taking long walks through the cornfields with her collie, Sam.